Mr Smith

MR SMITH
THE FAN WHO JOINED
THE IBROX LEGENDS

WALTER SMITH
with KEN GALLACHER

MAINSTREAM
PUBLISHING

EDINBURGH AND LONDON

First published in Great Britain in 1994 by
MAINSTREAM PUBLISHING COMPANY (EDINBURGH) LTD
7 Albany Street
Edinburgh EH1 3UG

ISBN 1 85158 668 7

A catalogue record for this book is available from the
British Library

Typeset in Palatino by Litho Link Ltd, Welshpool, Powys, Wales
Printed in Great Britain by Butler and Tanner Ltd, Frome

For Ethel and the boys, Neil and Steven,
for their support and love over the years and for
a much-loved grandfather, old Jock, who taught me to
support the best team in the world

Contents

CHAPTER ONE

A Shock Arrival at Ibrox

For most of my life I had dreamed of joining Rangers. As a kid, they were the team I wanted to play for. As a senior player, I always hoped that I might be good enough to get there. But I wasn't . . .

As a coach, I was almost there, along with Jim McLean when he had been offered the job. But he turned it down and after he had made his decision he told me that I was also staying on with Dundee United. That looked as if it would be my one and only chance. Until one day in February 1986 I received a phone call from a friend asking if I could meet him at the Gleneagles Hotel for a chat. And it was there I was told that Rangers wanted me to join up at Ibrox as assistant manager to Graeme Souness. I didn't hesitate over the offer. I said that I wanted the job and things began to move. What I didn't know then was the size of the job we were about to take on.

In those initial weeks after I was appointed, the move I had dreamed about all my life turned into a little bit of a nightmare. To be absolutely honest, the club was a shambles. The club I had admired for so long from the outside was just a shell, a ghost club which seemed to be rudderless, and drifting into a couldn't-care-less state that would have shocked the supporters. Of course, one of the first problems I had was that before I stepped into the job the directors in charge, Lawrence Marlborough and David Holmes, had sacked the entire backroom staff. That was done on the Monday and I went in the following day. Alone. Absolutely on my own because Graeme was still in Sampdoria and could not join the club for another month or so. It's difficult to realise now when you walk around Ibrox that I could have felt so much alone. Today, the club has grown and there are always people around. Back then it was a whole lot different!

When the players arrived that first morning I was there with the physiotherapist, Bob Findlay, trying to pick up on the way things were done at the club. You have to understand that at every club there are set routines regarding training and the way the kit is laid out and prepared, the way the first team and the reserves are split, all kinds of things which vary from club to club. At Dundee United the training gear was laid out ready for the arriving players. They went to their own pegs, changed there and went out to work. That morning at Ibrox, the players came in, took their gear from a pile which was sitting in the middle of the dressing-room, put it on and then went out to work. I watched and wondered, and then there was worse to come . . .

It was wet that morning, real Glasgow rain, and after training we went back across to the stadium, the players dumped their gear and we went upstairs for lunch, just as we still do, and then went home. After that I went back down to the dressing-room. The balls, old and scuffed, were lying around. The gear was still there in a sodden, muddy heap. The groundstaff lads – all two of them – had gone home. I knew then that I had a job on my hands to lick things into shape.

When the lads reported the following day the training gear had been put away on hangers into old-fashioned drying rooms. The trouble, though, was that none of it had been washed first. So what we had was dirty, muddy, stiff tracksuits. They were as hard as boards because they had been hung away when they were still wet. And still dirty. This seemed to be the way things were done at Ibrox and it appalled me. I looked at the players going out to training and I thought to myself: 'Rangers players should not look that way!'

At Tannadice it had never been like that. Not when I first went there as a young player, when Jerry Kerr was the manager. And certainly not in the later years of Jim McLean's rule. Back in my early days, the trainer, Andy Dickson, had been in charge of the kit and it was washed every day after training and every morning there was a fresh kit available for every player. Somehow, though, that didn't seem to have been a part of the Rangers way and it was something I knew we had to change.

I'd learned from Jim McLean that when you are trying to build something at a club you must look after the tiniest details. It always seems that if you can get these right then everything else can fall into place. We had to start doing that with Rangers. It was a case of going back to basics. That was not what I had expected. I had had a vision of Ibrox all my life, in which everything at the stadium was as near-perfect as you can get it at a football club.

But back then, for whatever reasons, the infrastructure of the club was not right. That had to be overhauled dramatically. I recognised, too, that the team had to be rebuilt. That was the main reason, after all, for Rangers appointing Graeme and me. Looking around now at the stadium, with the constant bustle, the people coming and going, the commercial department flourishing and the constant queues for tickets for games, I often think back to the empty, echoing marble halls which greeted me on my arrival. An arrival which had been delayed for two-and-a-half years . . .

Back in the autumn of 1983, after John Greig left the manager's office, Jim McLean was offered the job. At that time Rangers had tried to lure Alex Ferguson from Aberdeen and failed. Then they targeted wee Jim and he told me that he wanted me to go to Ibrox with him. He didn't ask me – that wasn't Jim's way – he just told me. My career was being shaped by him and because of my feeling for Rangers I was happy to go along with that.

I had had other offers – three to manage other clubs and one to be assistant to Alex Ferguson at Aberdeen. That would have been interesting, but I was enjoying my job at Tannadice, where we had been winning trophies and doing well in Europe. Motherwell asked me if I wanted to be the boss at Fir Park and St Johnstone and St Mirren both came in with bids to move me from Tannadice. I knocked all of them back and then Jim told me about Rangers and his offer from them.

When that offer arrived, he told me that we would both be going and, this time, there was never going to be any chance of a refusal on my part. He knew that without having to ask me. He kept me in touch with everything that was happening, even telling me that he was going to an interview in the Hampden carpark – well away from Ibrox so that news of the interview did not leak out.

After that meeting he drove back up to Dundee and came to see me to discuss the offer. He told me that the job was his and then asked me what I thought about the whole move. That was a hard one for me, and I had to say that to him. My view was that he should jump at the chance but, then, I was more than a little biased. We were talking about the club I'd supported as a boy, the club I'd always dreamed of joining. It was, I said, up to him to decide because my view was less than impartial. After some more talk he got up to go and said he was going to think about it overnight. It was obvious to me that he had some misgivings. What they were I didn't know. Even to this day I don't know. But they were there that night we talked and I felt that things might still go wrong for me. I always reckon that if you have to think about something like a job offer then maybe it's not the right one for you. And the more you do think about it, then the more problems, real or imagined, begin to surface.

However, at the start of that week – a day or two after the Hampden carpark meeting – he told me he was taking the job. Not only that, we were leaving Tannadice the following week. There were to be no delays, no hanging around, we were taking over at Ibrox immediately. He said that he had told the club chairman, Johnstone Grant, that we were both going. That was fine by me. I left everything to him and I was so convinced that it was all falling into place that I even phoned my old man to tell him what was happening.

Then on Friday morning there was a board meeting called at Tannadice. It sticks in my mind because, while there was a board meeting every Friday at the park, this one was called for ten o'clock instead of the usual midday. Jim was to make everything formal at this meeting and Gordon Wallace and myself were taking the training. There wasn't much involved in that. There never is on a Friday because that's the day before a game and all you tend to do is a little bit of track work and then let the players go home early. That day was a routine

Friday, except for the fact that most of the players knew what was going on and most of them recognised that the formalities were being settled in the board room while they were training.

I can recall going back into the dressing-room when most of the lads had gone home and there were only two players left there. One was Derek Johnstone, who was on loan to United from Chelsea at that time, and the other was Davie Dodds, who is now at Ibrox with me. Doddsy has always been a Rangers supporter. He is a Dundonian but somehow has always followed Rangers since he was at school. The two of them were sitting there and saying to me, 'Well, that's it, you'll be happy now you're off to Ibrox', and things like that. And I didn't want to say too much until wee Jim came downstairs and told me. So I sat there trying to say nothing at all to the two of them.

Then at five minutes to twelve one of the senior directors, George Fox, burst through the dressing-room door and looked around, thinking he would see most of the players there. Instead, only the three of us, me, big Derek and Doddsy were in the room. He recovered himself and then announced: 'Great news. Fabulous news. The manager's staying with the club!' Well, what was 'great news' for Mr Fox, and for Dundee United, was a shattering blow to me. I just sat there for a few minutes, got up, went into the shower and then afterwards drove straight home. I didn't speak to anyone. I didn't feel able to speak to anyone. The next day I turned up for the game as usual – I can't even remember now who we were playing – did what I had to do and all Jim told me was that he had felt that the right thing for him to do was stay where he was at Tannadice. He did not go into any more detail than that. He didn't give any real explanation as to why he turned the job down. And to this day he has still never elaborated to me on his reasons for staying with United.

As for me, I thought that was it. The dream had ended. You don't get too many chances to go to a club as big as Rangers. Wee Jim had been a dozen years or so working at Tannadice before the opportunity arrived for him. So it seemed a distant and remote possibility that I might ever be able to work at Ibrox.

It was a tough period we entered at Tannadice then. After winning the title and reaching the European Cup semi-final, we should have been able to freshen up the side a little. We needed to bring in new players, to try to get a better class of player to come to Tannadice, but we could not afford that. We had to work away with what we had and hope that some fresh young talent would come through from the reserves . . .

I just worked away and kept doing the job I had been doing for the past five years or so. Even today, when I think back, I can still feel the bitter sense of disappointment I felt at that time. I had to shove that into the background and get on with my job and my life but it changed my view of things. From then on I knew that if a decent job offer came I would have to take it. I was not going to be content to stay at Tannadice any longer . . . What I did not expect was a second chance to go to Ibrox.

I just feel fortunate now that no other job offer came up in that intervening spell because the whole affair had unsettled me. It had been a real blow and a hard thing to accept, especially as Jim had made the decision for me – though, to be fair, he knew that going to Rangers was always my ambition. Then when he changed his mind there was no real explanation as to why my life had been changed again. From then on I could not see myself continuing forever the way I had been doing at Tannadice.

I'm not a great believer in luck but circumstances do have a habit of shaping your life for you. You can, for example, go to a club at just the right time. Or, alternatively, you can avoid going to a club when it appears to be the wrong time to take over. In hindsight, I like to think that circumstances eventually favoured me and my career.

I do not believe I would have enjoyed the kind of success I have had at Rangers if I had come to the club with Jim McLean. At that time various things surrounding the club were different. There was a different board, whose members appeared to be less ambitious than the men who were in command when my second chance arrived. And Jim would have gone about the job in a far, far different way from the route chosen by Graeme Souness!

The only problem I had was that despite the fact that he had wanted to take me to Rangers himself, wee Jim didn't want me to leave this time when I had the chance to go on my own. When the news leaked he was far from happy. But, by then, I didn't care too much. I had committed myself. And I'd done it without having any great discussions with the man I was to work with over the next five hectic years – Graeme Souness.

I knew Graeme but I didn't know him well. Our acquaintance was limited to the few times I had been with the Scotland team in the build-up to the World Cup finals in Mexico. Before the finals, we were set to play a warm-up game in Glasgow against Romania, and it was then Graeme and I first talked about the job offers we had been given. At this stage it was all still under wraps. Few people knew what was going on behind the scenes. Anyway, Graeme asked me if I had been approached about joining Rangers and then confirmed that he had been asked to be player-manager. He wanted to know if I was willing to be his assistant manager. There was no great hesitation on my part. It was the club I wanted to join and he told me he felt the same way, and even then, at that first chat, I felt the chemistry between us was right.

I'm still amazed that the moves were kept so secret. That's unusual in football but this time the handful of people in on the secret remained tight-lipped. Whilst I waited for the final moves to be made, the club itself was being restructured. Lawrence Marlborough had taken control and he was drafting in David Holmes as his chairman. Then, one night when Rangers were playing a friendly at Ibrox against Tottenham Hotspur, I met David Holmes in the Pond Hotel and he outlined the job on offer and I agreed to take it.

It was only after I left him that I realised I hadn't even asked what my salary was going to be! I suppose that indicates just how much I wanted to go to Ibrox. From then on things moved swiftly. Rangers worked out a settlement with their then manager, Jock Wallace, and announced that Graeme was taking over as player-manager. And the rumours then began that I was going to be the number two and Jim McLean duly called me into his office at Tannadice one morning and asked me what was going to happen.

I'd been 20 years with the man by then and there was no way I was going to start telling him any lies. I told him that I had been approached and that the job was there for me and that I wanted to take it. He countered that by saying that Rangers were 'poaching' me, quite forgetting that he had done the same thing two-and-a-half years earlier. When he was approached, he had asked me to go with him!

I couldn't understand why he was taking this attitude. Then in mid-April I went into Tannadice to take training and he called me into his office again and said that Rangers had now made an official request, asking to talk to me, and that United had agreed, 'reluctantly', to allow the meeting to go ahead. That same afternoon I was down in Glasgow in David Holmes's office with Graeme, who had flown in from Genoa for the meeting. It was then that I found out that United were still putting barriers in my way. They now said that they wanted to keep me at Tannadice for a little longer. Rangers wanted me the very next day!

They also said that they wanted a fee of £50,000 for me. I found that ridiculous. As a player, Jim had once sold me to Dumbarton for just £7,000 and bought me back for three grand less! My value had shot up sensationally over the years. To be honest, I didn't think they had any right to ask for that kind of compensation for me and I told David Holmes that. But I was then given an insight into how my life would be with Rangers.

David Holmes picked up the phone and called George Fox. He had a speaker switched on so that I could hear the entire conversation and he simply asked him where the £50,000 cheque had to be sent. When he was told to send the money to George Fox's house, he sat down and wrote out the cheque in front of me, summoned a courier and had it delivered to Carnoustie that evening. That cleared the decks for me to start the job immediately.

I was happy at that but far from happy at the way Dundee United had more or less held Rangers to ransom. That hurt me at the time, though the hurt has faded with the years. But, then, I looked at the 20 years I had given to the club. Twenty years without any trouble, 20 years when I felt I had always given the club 100 per cent, and that wasn't taken into consideration. With another club that demand might have cost me the chance of the job. If the boot had been on the other foot

United would never have forked out that kind of compensation. I know that.

It was my first illustration of the difference between working for a small club and working for a major club. It made a big impression on me. It might have been a sad way to end my time at Tannadice but it also underlined to me just how much value Rangers were placing on me and that positive attitude outweighed the petty-minded stance United adopted in those weeks of negotiation. I can still remember John Paton asking me later if United had given me any of that cash as a golden handshake. They hadn't and it had never crossed my mind that they would even make the offer. But if they had done, I would have knocked it back – that's how upset I was at the time. All I wanted then was to get on with the new job, the new career and the same old task – trying to guide the team into Europe over the last few fateful weeks of that season.

When I arrived at Ibrox the team had just lost to bottom-of-the-table Clydebank by 2–1 at Kilbowie Park. Confidence was anything but high and Dundee were closing in on the club in the battle for a UEFA place. The first game I had in charge was against St Mirren at Love Street and we lost again – once more, the score was 2–1. Europe was drifting out of reach with only two games remaining, and one of these was up at Pittodrie against Alex Ferguson's team, who had already beaten Rangers twice that season and drawn the third game. Our last match, and our last chance for Europe, was to be against Motherwell at home. The defeat by St Mirren had handed Graeme and I our first Ibrox crisis – I'd been at the club less than a week and Graeme hadn't even joined up yet. Those early worrying days gave us an insight into what it was going to be like . . .

There is never a time at Ibrox when you can relax. There is never a time when you can sit back and say to yourself that everything is just perfect. Because there are always demands for improvement and in those first weeks we learned that. It wasn't our team, the players were not chosen by us, but somehow we had to get the utmost from them to make sure that the future, the immediate future, was going to include European football. That was essential to our ambitions.

Ted McMinn scored for us at Aberdeen and, although John Hewitt equalised, we were able to get a draw. In the last match, against Motherwell, we won 2–0 with goals from Dave McPherson and Ally McCoist. It was enough – just enough – to get us into Europe. Dundee, who were being managed by Archie Knox then, finished on the same points total as we did but we had a far superior goal difference.

The team had been on a downer when we arrived and all the changes had caused more upset. They took just four points from their last seven League games – and three of them were in those last two matches. It was in those final weeks of the season that I realised just how big a task we had taken on. The behind-the-scenes problems that I touched on at the start of this chapter had to be remedied.

By this time I'd had a close look at the playing staff. Knowing the playing standards that had been set at Tannadice with Dundee United, I knew what standard of player we should be looking at for the kind of club Graeme and I wanted Rangers to become. It was obvious that we did not have enough of the quality players we would need, and I told Graeme that. There had never been any doubt that Rangers needed an injection of fresh talent. We had both agreed on that but you always hope that there are players on the staff who will surprise you, younger players you don't know a lot about, perhaps. But while there were one or two, there were nowhere near enough to give us the basis of the powerful squad we knew we needed.

Still, there was some reason for hope. And that arrived on the last day of the season. It was a Friday night and we had a Glasgow Cup game to play at Ibrox against Celtic. It was the first taste of the Old Firm clashes for both Graeme and me – and while it was only a Glasgow Cup game, we desperately wanted to win it. Celtic had taken the title the previous weekend and we knew our fans wanted a result from us. We got it. A hat-trick from Ally McCoist was enough for a 3–2 win at a sell-out Ibrox and the fans left happy and we had been given a taste of things to come.

That was the start of it, the start of the Rangers revolution.

CHAPTER TWO

Come the Revolution . . .

I believe now that Graeme and I needed the twin boost that we received in the dying days of that season just after we had been appointed. Qualifying for the UEFA Cup when it had seemed to be slipping beyond the reach of the club was a major bonus for the next season – our first full season in charge.

Winning that Old Firm game gave us the breathing space we needed from the immediate demands made by the support. It might be only a Glasgow Cup game to the rest of the world, but to Old Firm fans it was much, much more. Playing that game against Celtic, and winning that game, let both Graeme and I know the value placed on the derby fixture by both sets of supporters! It told us something else, too, about this sleeping giant we had been placed in charge of. It told us the power that the fans could generate and demonstrated to the pair of us just what could be done if we turned things round.

The great thing about Graeme was that he came into the job as Rangers manager with few preconceived ideas about the job and about the club than most of us in Scotland would have had. Having been away from home for so long, Graeme saw Rangers not simply as a great Scottish institution – he saw Rangers as a great club in a British context. Or even in a European context. He was, therefore, not inhibited by the fact that Rangers happened to play north of the border in a country which was often written off by the English as a football power. He looked at the club, looked at the potential, saw the massive support which was available, and then decided that when we brought new players to the club nothing but the best would be good enough. Whereas anyone getting the job who had a totally Scottish background would have looked around the Premier League only, Graeme went for the top players in England!

He talked things over with me and we decided the areas where the team had to be strengthened, and then we started to look at the players who might be available for us to buy. We wanted a big, powerful centre-forward. We went for Colin West at Watford and we signed him – he was the first player we bought and he cost us £175,000, which was soon going to look like chickenfeed once Graeme had warmed to his task!

But what the signing told the football world was that Graeme was not going to be confined to Scotland in his bid to resurrect Rangers. He had his own ideas on how the game should be played – he always did want a target man up front – and if he felt that he would get better value for his money in England then that's where he would do his shopping. Apart from the fact that he had such a good knowledge of the English game after his years with Liverpool, he learned early that rival clubs in Scotland were not going to be happy to sell Rangers players. Two enquiries for Richard Gough at Tannadice which were made very early in our time at Ibrox were rejected out of hand. Just as I had predicted. That underlined Graeme's determination to concentrate on cross-border raids which could bring him the quality players he wanted.

Very soon it became obvious that Terry Butcher was to leave Ipswich and immediately he became a prime target for us. Then, we heard on the grapevine that Chris Woods wanted to join us. Here we were, a few weeks into the job and getting ready to buy two of England's World Cup stars as they prepared to head for the finals in Mexico! It was unheard of. Top English players simply didn't come to Scotland to ply their trade. They had their own big clubs and all the time they were being told that our Premier League was a second-rate affair. Graeme was going to change all of that. Dramatically!

Life, however, was complicated as we tried to put our plans into operation that summer. The World Cup finals were taking place in Mexico and both Graeme and myself were with the Scotland squad. I was there as Alex Ferguson's assistant, while Graeme was still captain of the Scotland side. Our two targets, Terry and Woodsy, were with England. It was a long, drawn-out hunt. Both countries went to the United States for altitude training – we were in Santa Fe while the English lads were in Colorado Springs. That took two weeks out of the summer before the matches kicked off. Then we had the games, and in all that time we could not do anything to clinch either of the deals.

Graeme and I talked about our plans. We had to do that because we had left Ibrox deserted for the summer and there was no changing that. Still, we talked and we planned and always we came back to the same worrying thing that we could lose out on Terry Butcher because of the delay. Ipswich had accepted our offer of £750,000 and we knew we could speak to the player when his England commitments were fulfilled. But other major clubs were also waiting in the wings and I began to have doubts about whether Graeme's audacious move for the England star would pay off.

Graeme, though, being Graeme, didn't have the slightest worry about being able to persuade Terry to come north. Like thousands of Rangers fans, Graeme believed quite simply that he was with one of the greatest clubs in Britain. Therefore, he reasoned, it's a club which must be able to attract the best players. That view of the club has not always prevailed in, say, the south-east of England, but that little matter was not going to deflect Graeme. Terry Butcher was the man he wanted and Terry Butcher was going to be the man he fashioned his new-look Rangers around. By now he had made up his mind on that one. Of course, Manchester United had now declared an interest and that was going to complicate things a little if we did not get to the player first. Graeme, though, took care of that little matter as only he could . . .

After the World Cup was over Terry was asked to play in a special charity game in Los Angeles involving star players who had taken part in the matches in Mexico, including Gordon Strachan from the Scottish side. It was organised by UNICEF, I think, and the big man went to the west coast of the United States from his holiday with his family in Florida. After that game he was jetting straight back to London, ready to decide on his future. Graeme was at the airport when he stepped off the flight. He talked to him at one of the airport hotels and then, before Terry had had a chance to get back to Ipswich too see his wife and family, he had him on a shuttle to Glasgow.

Graeme could be very persuasive. Terry had been flying all night. He had been on that plane for eight or nine hours and yet, here he was, being whisked up to Glasgow to talk over a transfer. He went to Ibrox straight from the airport, looked at the ground, listened

This must remind Walter of his first days at Ibrox when he found himself on his own with no back-up . . . here the Boss is left collecting the cones after a training stint

When Walter Smith was a schooloy – and even before that – these gates at Ibrox were the entrance to his dreams. He is the Rangers fan who made it

A delighted Walter Smith with the three major domestic trophies which make up the Scottish 'treble' – the League Championship trophy, the Scottish Cup and the League Cup

Manager Smith in the Ibrox directors' box with chairman David Murray – the man, Smith reveals, who puts the vital finishing touches to the major transfer deals for Rangers

Advice from the touchline as Walter shouts instructions, watched by Andy Goram on the bench and coach Davie Dodds standing at the right

Smith faces the European press during Rangers' undefeated run in the European Champions League

Defender Richard Gough, who skippered Rangers to their record-breaking triumphs but who began his career with Walter Smith at Dundee United

*Stuart McCall was one of the first signings made by Walter as he began
to rebuild the side after the departure of Graeme Souness*

*Walter Smith takes a close look at goalkeeper Andy Goram – he says that
in an 18-month period Goram didn't make a single mistake!*

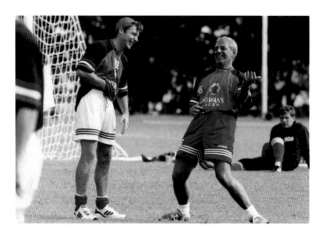

Just how can you stay serious when striker Ally McCoist is around? Boss Smith cracks up with the Ibrox star at pre-season training in Italy

Now the Gaffer tries to get serious – but the smiles are not far away

Ally gets the last laugh as the Boss gets his point over!

Things get serious on the training ground in this three-way talk-in between assistant manager Archie Knox, manager Smith and midfield international star Stuart McCall

Walter Smith is confirmed as Rangers manager by chairman David Murray, though the decision had been made in secret much earlier than the official press conference

*One-million-pound man Mark Hateley, who developed into one of
Rangers' best-ever buys, in Walter Smith's opinion*

*He was only Number Two to Graeme Souness in this dug-out scene, but
Walter Smith still put his point across – forcibly! Beside him are defender
John Brown and former club physio Phil Boersma*

to Graeme outline his plans to make Rangers a major force in the game and then arranged for his wife to fly up the next day. By then, Graeme was sure that he had landed his man – and he was right. Terry signed and, at the time, I knew that this was a very special signing for us. I wasn't thinking solely in terms of his ability and his leadership qualities then, I was thinking of just how much it raised the profile of our club. That signing, plus the fact that Chris Woods was also going to join us, pushed us straight in among the major transfer-market players in the whole of Britain.

It was what we needed then. And as the seasons rolled by, the value of that signing was emphasised to all of us at the club over and over again. The two players, too, were an astonishing bargain for us. We were getting England's World Cup captain and their number two keeper – only kept out of the side by Peter Shilton, remember – for £1.2m. I doubt that we ever did a better bit of business than that double summer signing. We were on our way into an area of the game which the major English clubs had thought would remain their exclusive preserve.

After years of Scottish sides being plundered by the giants of the First Division we were striking back. Their top players were coming to Scotland. And it was all down to Graeme Souness – let no one ever believe otherwise! Graeme reversed that trend. He changed things round. Suddenly Rangers had two of *England's* top players and that was a situation no one would ever have believed in all the seasons which went before. And the moves paid off for us . . .

There is no doubt that we would have liked to bring in more players, especially as Colin West was injured in the first League Cup tie of the season, against East Fife, and was out of the side for months after that. But we went into the season with only *three* major acquisitions: Graeme himself, who was player-manager, Terry and Woodsy. The reason for that was simple – at the time we didn't have any more money. We could not afford to bring in another class player. Although we were to spend far more money in the years which lay ahead, we had reached our limit with those first important transfers. That's why it was so important to Graeme and me, as well as to the club, that the signings we made were the *right* signings.

It turned out that they were the men for the job. We all got a tremendous lift from the performances they gave week after week and from the way the crowds took to them. The response was fantastic, far better than we had ever dreamed. The crowds soared and all around Ibrox there was a feeling of real optimism, where in previous seasons there had been only pessimism. The signings we made gave the support hope for the future and as the results were strung together they all began to realise that their hope was not misplaced. Of course, also, we were giving the fans new faces, new stars, players they were accustomed to seeing only on the telly or in big international matches. Now they were playing for *their* team, for Rangers, week after week.

There were people who claimed that the potential was always there for Rangers to do this kind of thing. Maybe it had been there, simmering in the background but ignored by the men who had previously run the club. Who knows for sure? What we do know is that Graeme turned it into reality. He brought all the dreams alive.

He was the catalyst for change, backed by David Holmes, who was determined to put the club on the map. I remain convinced, though, that without Graeme it would not have happened. He *knew* these players; they *knew* him. They had played against him and they had seen him win trophy after trophy with Liverpool and then take his talents to Sampdoria, and they recognised that if Graeme Souness was ready to continue his career in Scotland then it was always going to be worth while joining forces with him!

Once Graeme had been put in place, and then followed up his own appointment by recruiting the first two England international stars, then Rangers, because of the size of the club, could handle the rest. You have also got to remember that both Terry Butcher and Chris Woods came from much smaller clubs even though they were in the English First Division. Neither Ipswich nor Norwich could attract the crowds or inspire the passion that was on tap in Glasgow. Thinking it over now, you have to say that maybe the club should have been handling that kind of talent before but until Graeme came on the scene it had never been attempted.

It was a brilliant time to be there. Hectic, but almost always rewarding. We had some problems in bedding in the new players, just as any team does when there is a turnover in personnel because as you alter the team you cannot always get the level of consistency you enjoyed when the side was settled. In our case, we also had to get the players who had been with the club before our arrival into our way of playing the game. We had to get them on to the same wavelength as ourselves and all of this takes time.

We were helped by our victory in the League Cup late in October in an Old Firm final at Hampden. We won 2–1 that day with goals from Ian Durrant and Davie Cooper and that trophy gave us the momentum to go for the Premier League title. Until then we had been toiling a little bit, struggling to find the level of form we knew we needed to win a Championship. That's why it was a bonus for us that the Cup-winning goals came from two of the lads who had been with the club for some time. And these two flourished in the new environment. We were learning quite quickly that in Durrant we had someone who could prove to be an exceptional player, while Davie Cooper was simply fabulous. To a large extent, in the troubled years that Rangers had gone through Coop had been asked to carry the weight of the fans' expectations. He had been their star player, their one hope for glory, if you like, and the pressure on him must have been enormous. I believe that it might have soured him a little and affected his performances. Too much was expected from one man. Now that burden moved away from Coop, and Souness, Butcher and Woods had to take their share of that heavy, heavy load. That allowed Coop the freedom to play, it gave him the setting he needed and he responded. For my money, Davie Cooper could have featured in any team you care to name. He was a magnificent footballer.

But, because of what was happening at the club, we got a lift from other players, too. Coisty, always a goalscorer, was doing his bit. Lads like Cammy Fraser and Jimmy Nicholl contributed and big Dave McPherson played alongside Terry and looked solid and comfortable . . . It was as if the other players saw things happening at the club that they never believed would happen. They got the message that this was the start of something big and there was a response from all of them. That helped make our job easier . . . though, as always, you need a little bit of luck along the way.

For example, I can remember Robert Fleck getting himself into bother at an Old Firm reserve game and Graeme deciding that he had to go. We just thought that Flecky was not going to do it for us and with that incident hanging over him as well it was the right time to let him go elsewhere. So Graeme and I talked it over and we knew that it was not going to be easy to get a lot of money for a player who was, basically, a reserve. That's when I said I would phone Jocky Scott, who was the manager of Dundee at the time and who was looking for a front man. Inevitably, Jocky's problem was that he didn't have any money. And I mean *any* money. Graeme and I spoke about his problem and we dropped the price as low as twenty grand. Still, Jocky could not come up with enough – and that's where luck came into it. A year or so later Flecky had a run in the first team, Norwich liked what they saw and Graeme did finally sell him – for £600,000. We were almost caught with that one because there is always the chance when a club is in turmoil that you can make that kind of mistake about a player. It almost happened to us but luck was with us that time.

Going back to that first season, we needed the lift that the League Cup win gave us and after that, coming up towards mid-season, we were able to buy Graham Roberts from Spurs, and he brought some more stability to the defensive side of our game. Anyhow, we suffered in the Scottish Cup, with a defeat at the hands of Hamilton Accies in the first round proper – and it came at Ibrox. But somehow we had kept ourselves in the title race and we went up to Pittodrie on the second-last day of the season, had Graeme sent off, and yet clinched the title. It was an unforgettable climax to our first season in charge and it told us again just how much the Rangers fans had missed success. This was the first title win they could celebrate in nine long, empty years. It was almost unbelievable that a huge club like Rangers, with that massive support and tremendous resources, could have been out in the cold for so long.

What it meant for Graeme and me was that we had been able to deliver the trophies we had been hired to win. We had gone out in Europe in the third round of the UEFA Cup to the German side Borussia Moenchengladbach in a tie we might have won. And we had gone out of the Scottish Cup in that disastrous match with Hamilton. But we had been able to get victory in the League Cup and a title victory which had left Celtic eventually trailing us by six points. Now the harsher realities of life with Rangers began to hit us in that close-season. After the euphoria, after all the celebrations had died down, we had to look at the squad again and decide the next stage in the development of the club. We knew we now had the fans with us. The first year had proved that a successful Rangers team would draw huge crowds to Ibrox.

But we had to build on the success we had had. With a top club you cannot sit back and wallow in the celebrations which mark your trophy wins. You have to be thinking ahead, and the main aim must always be to try to improve the team while you are still winning. Our problem was that at the end of that season we did not get the quality of new signings we were looking for. We brought in Avi Cohen, an old team-mate of Graeme's from Liverpool, and Trevor Francis, who had played with Graeme at Sampdoria. And Mark Falco had come in from Watford . . . but we had not been able to sign the star names we had produced the previous summer: Trevor and Avi were reaching the latter stages of their careers and Graeme himself was beginning to bow out of the playing side. Then, in a League game against Aberdeen at Ibrox, Terry Butcher broke his leg, and suddenly we were up against it. Just before that leg break we had managed to get Richard Gough back from Spurs – now instead of Goughie adding to the depth of the first-team squad he simply became a replacement for Terry. Richard had been signed a month earlier and he and Butcher had only managed four games together before Terry broke his leg.

Again, we were able to lift the League Cup, winning on penalties against Aberdeen after a marvellous final which ended in a 3–3 draw. That allowed us breathing space but we were never able to get back the momentum we had built up in our first season. Basically, we were not nearly as good as we wanted to be. The standard of player at the club did drop in that second season and we went back almost to square one. When we were faced with long-term injuries, such as the one to Terry Butcher, we found ourselves in bother.

It was to be towards the middle and then even later in the season that we were able to re-group and construct the kind of player-pool we wanted to keep together for a longer period of time. More money had to be spent. The directors, led by David Holmes, the chairman, made that available and so we embarked on the second wave of spending.

What the second year showed us early on was that things won't just happen for you – you have to get out there and make them happen. And it demonstrated to me right away that there was never any time for relaxation. That's why we began the push for players towards the turn of the year. Ray Wilkins came in from Paris for a bargain fee of £150,000 and proved one of the most astute signings we ever made. At New Year we bought Mark Walters in a bid to add width to the side. Then, towards the end of the season, John Brown and Ian Ferguson were signed. We lost the League – in fact, we finished third – but we had a growing belief in the squad of players we had now been able to put together. There was no consolation in the Scottish Cup either – that jinx remained hanging over us. Although we got through the first round this time, it was scarcely a glorious victory – we drew with Raith Rovers at Starks Park before beating them in the Ibrox replay. Then in the next round we returned to Fife and Dunfermline knocked us out . . .

The League Cup apart, the only bright spots for us were in the European Cup even though that, too, ended in disaster. We beat Dynamo Kiev in the first round, knocked out the Polish champions Gornik in the second round and then went out 3–2 on aggregate to Steaua Bucharest from Romania in the quarter-finals.

In the summer we added Gary Stevens, another England regular, and striker Kevin Drinkell to produce one of our most powerful squads. There were times in that season when we played quite brilliant football. We were desperately close to winning the 'treble' that year. It was a good time for us at the club . . . even though the previous season had ended in disappointment. There was also some unwelcome publicity over a dressing-room row involving Graham Roberts, Graeme Souness and myself. That caused us a few problems at the club and with the supporters, who had turned Robbo into a kind of cult figure at Ibrox. But, in the end, we had no choice but to put him up for sale. After our second-last game of the season, when we had lost to Aberdeen, he questioned our authority in the dressing-room and, later, publicly. Once that had happened there was no way back for him. It didn't matter to us whether or not the fans wanted him to stay. If one player, just a single player, is allowed to get away with something like that then others will follow and you cannot have that happen in any dressing-room. That can lead to all kinds of trouble and we had to nip it in the bud.

The rumours swept around Glasgow after the bust-up. Robbo and Graeme were supposed to have thrown punches, but nothing like that ever happened. In fact, it all started off with me when I questioned

Graham's positioning when we lost one of the goals that day. He refused to accept any blame when it was clear to everyone in the dressing-room that he had been at fault. In the middle of this Graeme walked in. Very few words were spoken between them. Not too many were necessary. He had to go: popular player or not, there was no longer any place for him at the club.

We simply could not have our authority being undermined at that time, especially as we were going through such a poor spell on the field. But Robbo didn't see things from our point of view; or maybe he just didn't want to take another look. Anyhow, at Falkirk on the following Saturday, the last Premier League game of the season, he turned up and took his seat in the stand among the punters. He was cheered to his seat and, on the bench, Graeme and I were barracked. The jeers spread to the chairman in the stand and it was not a happy time for us. But now that he is doing a bit on the management side himself, I'm sure Graham Roberts realises that the outcome was inevitable. Going to Brockville didn't help his case any – but the decision had been made. Graeme and I had discussed it and while we knew the decision to sell him would not be popular we also knew it was a decision we could not afford to shirk.

Managers cannot afford to walk away from difficult or unpopular judgments. Often things happen away from the public gaze which determine the direction you take. But if you bottle a tough disciplinary matter then you can lose *all* the players, not just the one who brought the trouble to a head.

That was only one of the decisions we had to take which were not popular, but I was in agreement with Graeme over all the major policies which were adopted on the playing side at the club. We had started off in the job not really knowing each other very well. But over the five years we were together I like to think that we developed a good, strong working relationship and a friendship which continues to this day.

Perhaps the working circumstances we were thrown into were a little different from most managers and their assistants. But, always, Graeme was the manager. I don't believe in the 'joint-manager' thing. You have to have one man whose word is final and in this case Graeme had that last word. I still reckon it has to be that way. Not that it brought any major clashes between the two of us. We discussed everything and, while we did not always agree, we were, for most of the time, on the same wavelength.

As far as the organisation at the grass-roots level was concerned, the nuts and bolts of running a football club, if you like, I had most of the responsibility for that. Graeme, after all, was coming to that side of it cold. He had played the game at the very highest level but he had not been asked to put together training routines or set up a backroom staff and lay out their various duties. I had had eight years' experience on the management side with Dundee United and so I took all that on board.

But when it came to the first team, we had long discussions about the various aspects – about the players we might want to buy and the ones we might want to move on – and always in these discussions Graeme was the man with the final judgment.

In all that time I cannot recall one major falling-out between us. It was a partnership I look back on with affection because I gained a lot from it. There were a lot of times when we found ourselves under scrutiny by the media. Times when the decisions which were taken were not popular with the support. Or with the players. Or, very often, with the football authorities. And universally unpopular with the fans of every other club in the country. That was never something which worried Graeme. And, gradually, it was not something which worried me either. We were different personalities but on major issues we were in agreement. And if what we did regarding any matter involving the club was unpopular, then that's just the way it had to be. We did whatever we had to do to keep Rangers at the top. Anything we did was done for what we saw as the good of the club. We both realised that we were in football to win games, to win trophies if possible, and not to win any popularity contests. A manager has to have the strength of character to handle all of that and I think we both faced up to the responsibilities.

It was an exciting time then. A good time to be with Rangers and I wouldn't swap that period for anything. Yes, we had our troubles, but they were far outweighed by the job we did. Poor Graeme was the main focus for the jealousies which surfaced and the main focus for trouble, too. People have said to me since that I was a good partner for him to have around because I could be a restraining influence on him. When I think about that one I guess I didn't do a very good job. He managed to get himself into so much trouble that I couldn't have been much of a restraining influence on him at all!

But my times with him were unforgettable. Frantic. Furious. Fiery. The stormiest period of my football life and yet I was sad when they came to an end and Graeme left for Liverpool – even though I was handed the manager's job.

CHAPTER THREE

Graeme Goes – And The Job Is Mine!

Graeme Souness was probably the most volatile and controversial character I have ever been involved with. He is probably one of the most talked-about managers in Scotland because of what he set in motion atIbrox . . .

When he agreed to take the job as manager of Rangers he was front-page news. And back page. And inside the papers, too. Typically, when he left three years ago, he did so in the same blaze of publicity which had heralded his arrival. It was typical of the constant hype which had surrounded Graeme and the club that it would be that way. Typical, too, that Ibrox would be swamped in a sea of rumours about his successor within minutes of the official announcement that Graeme was going to return to his beloved Anfield as the new boss of Liverpool.

That was the way things had always been in the five years we had been together at the club. There was little point in thinking that it would all suddenly change when Graeme made up his mind to move on. This time round, though, I expected a blaze of publicity. I had become used to the club being the focus of constant media attention. And, I had had time to gear myself towards the situation when the news finally exploded, because Graeme had taken me into his confidence some months beforehand.

Nothing had happened suddenly. Nothing had been cobbled together in a rush. No one else had been seriously considered by the Liverpool board because Graeme had been approached by them as early as February. At least two months before it all became public, the initial sounding-out moves had been made and Graeme had kept me in touch all the way through the different stages of the long, complicated and difficult negotiations. It was a move which was on and then off, and then back on again as Graeme wrestled over an offer which was to change his life.

I can still remember when he first broached the subject with me. At that time major renovations were taking place at the stadium. The club deck was being built and the dressing-rooms were out of commission, and after training we were in the habit of going across to the nearby Bellahouston Hotel to take a sauna at the health club there. So, one day, there we were in the sauna and he suddenly hit me with the news that he had been offered the Liverpool job after Kenny Dalglish had resigned. Right after telling me, he asked me what I thought about it, and when he did that I began to realise that he was seriously considering going back to Anfield. I knew him well enough to recognise that he would never have asked me that question unless he was thinking it over. If he had had no interest then he would have rejected the offer out of hand and I would never have known about it until well after the event.

At the same time, I could sense that, perhaps, he had some doubts, some misgivings over the move and that's why he was asking me for my opinion. I was a bit taken aback and I didn't say too much to him about it right at that moment. It was the next day, after I had given the affair some serious thought myself, that I ventured an opinion. The most obvious thing to me was that there would be an emotional pull which Graeme would find attractive, going back to the scene of so many of his triumphs as a player and all of that. But there was going to be much more to any move than that alone. So I said to him : 'That's not an easy job you have been offered. You have to look at it that way before you make up your mind. You are going to go back to a place which you remember as having a certain standard of football, a certain quality of player and almost non-stop success. Now Kenny has left and one of his biggest problems has been trying to replace himself. And replacing so many of the lads who were there with the two of you in the club's best years. It's a really difficult one.' As well as that, I pointed out to him that he might have to tread on a lot of toes – which turned out to be the case – if he was to get the team going again and return to the times he had played through and remembered now so affectionately.

It was fairly obvious, even to an outside eye, that there were players – some of whom Graeme had played with – who were coming to the end of their careers. It was going to be very, very difficult to go in there and make decisions which might be the right ones, but which would certainly be unpopular. With players. And with fans. You were, after all, looking at some players who had been magnificent servants for the club over the years, talented lads, not just ordinary players.

I don't know if what I said to him influenced him at all. He didn't say. All he told me a few days later was that he had turned the job down. Probably my views didn't affect him, because Graeme was never the kind of person to duck out of a challenge. Either as a player out on the field, or as a manager in his office, or as a man going through life. He always met any challenges head on. But this time, for whatever reasons, he said he was going to stay with Rangers. I thought the matter was over then and I was happy at that and ready to get on with the job we had to do at Ibrox.

Then, a few weeks later, we were on a plane to London, where we were going to watch a game, when Graeme suddenly told me that Liverpool had come back in for him. He didn't offer an explanation but it was fairly clear what had happened. Graeme had been their first choice and he had turned them down. Subsequently, they had looked around at other possible candidates, hadn't seen anyone around who matched up to Graeme and so they came all the way back to their first choice. This time Graeme didn't ask me for my opinion. He didn't take time to discuss it with me at all. On that flight south he simply told me that he had taken the job. I knew right away that there was no point in trying to talk him out of the move. The one sure thing I had learned in the five-year partnership was that when Graeme made up his mind then that was it. There was no going back. Also, Liverpool had talked him round and he had, by now, given them his word, and he would not go back on that.

In any case, within a few minutes it became more and more obvious to me that he was already making plans for his take-over at Anfield. For instance, he came straight out and asked me if I would move with him. I told him that I didn't want to go, but as I said that I realised that Graeme was so committed there was no going back for him. He asked me to keep silent about the whole thing and I agreed. It was his business and he had to handle it as he saw fit.

After that, he met the Liverpool people a couple of times and still everything remained under wraps, and then he told me that he was going to tell the chairman that he was leaving. He asked me again if I wanted to go with him. By then I'd looked at things over a period of time and I knew my initial reaction was the right one. I didn't want to leave Rangers. I'd spent a whole career trying to get to the club and there was no reason now to walk away from Ibrox. Going beyond that, I could see problems for anyone going to Liverpool as an assistant manager in charge of coaching and all the other duties I had at Ibrox. Liverpool had their own men, the lads in the fabled 'Boot Room', men such as Ronnie Moran and Roy Evans who had been there since Bill Shankly's time. They had their own ways, the Liverpool ways, the ways that had remained largely unchanged over the decades of success the club had known. I could never see them welcoming new blood, or wholesale changes in the way they did things. Nor would I have blamed them for that. Why should they change a system of training that had been the envy of so many other clubs in Britain and right across Europe?

But the bottom-line reason for me was that my heart was at Ibrox and that was not going to change. What Graeme wanted to do was his affair but no matter how much I had enjoyed the rollercoaster years working with him I just didn't want to leave Rangers. To be fair to him, he understood that and accepted it. Until he, or Liverpool, made things public we had to go on working as normal with the players as we tried to set up yet another Championship victory.

During the two or three weeks after he had told me of his decision and before the news leaked out, Graeme must have been under considerable personal pressure. There must have been tremendous inner turmoil, and yet he hid that from everyone. Not a single player suspected anything. No one at the club had a clue as to what was going on. Graeme went about his job in his normal way. He remained totally focused on the job he was doing at Ibrox and, for me, watching him, it was amazing how he was able to concentrate his mind the way he did. I admired that immensely – but I admired it alone, because no one else was yet in on the secret!

All of this was happening just when we had a little bit of a crisis on our hands. The side had been struck by a series of injuries which had interrupted the consistency of team selection we had been aiming for. As an obvious and inevitable consequence, our form had slipped and we were struggling for results. We were having to battle in every game just to get the points we needed to sustain our challenge for another Championship.

It was an awkward time for Graeme, and for me, too. The one person who finally suspected something was the chairman. Graeme had, for some reason or another, put off telling him. Probably because there was a personal friendship as well as a professional relationship involved. Then, one day, he said to me that he was going to tell the chairman on the coming Friday night; they had regular Friday night meetings over dinner, and it was going to be done then. But 24 hours before that the chairman called me at home, which was a bit unusual at that time. Out of the blue he asked me straight away: 'Do you know about Graeme going to Liverpool?' I was taken aback and admitted that Graeme had talked to me about it, and the chairman said simply: 'I sussed it!' I reckon that because they were so close the chairman had recognised that there was something more than just injury worries troubling Graeme at that period. So that Thursday Graeme sat down with the chairman and told him exactly what was happening. To be fair to Graeme, he had wanted to keep it quiet as long as possible because ideally he wanted to stay until the end of the season, see through the job he had, and then start fresh in the manager's job at Anfield.

The problem was that Liverpool didn't want that. They had their own worries at that time, and what they wanted was to announce the appointment as quickly as possible and then have Graeme come in to start the rebuilding which they must have believed was necessary. They were under fire from the fans too to make an appointment and I suppose they wanted to let them see that they had not been dragging their heels since Kenny walked out of the job. That was only to be expected . . .

But it didn't make things any easier for Rangers. Even when the news broke that Graeme was to go to Liverpool, he still wanted to stay on to complete the job he had started with Rangers. Knowing the injury worries which were damaging our title hopes, he wanted to stay and help. He was never a man to leave anyone in the lurch.

The chairman, though, made up his mind very quickly on that one. He said that Graeme had to go immediately. It was the right decision to make. I saw that as a time when the chairman had the opportunity to show his leadership – and he took it with both hands! It was a brave decision to make, but it was also correct and the supporters thought so too. Nevertheless, it presented problems we could have done without. Graeme's departure put everything up in the air at a time when we were all feeling under pressure in the dressing-room. It wasn't exactly the time we would have chosen for a change of manager.

The headlines when the story broke were enormous. The speculation surrounding Graeme's resignation and about who might now take over from him was unceasing. And there was I at the centre of it all – at the eye of the storm, if you like. I asked to see the chairman almost immediately to find out what my own future would be. I had already told him that I was staying with the club and that I had turned down the chance to go with Graeme to Liverpool. But I still wanted to know, from him, what my position would now be. At that initial meeting he asked me to carry on as normal – or as normally as possible in the circumstances – and to give him time to think things through. That was understandable. After all, he had not known as long as I had what was going on and he did need time to take it all in, to come to terms with Graeme's departure.

But he did tell me that there was every indication that he would ask me to take over. He asked me if I wanted the job but that was an unnecessary question. The chance of getting the manager's job with Rangers was so important to me that it would have beaten any other job offer I could ever get. But I realised that the chairman had to have some time to think things over . . .

He didn't take as long as I imagined he would. The following day he was at Ibrox for the game and he walked down the tunnel with me and we stood there together at the edge of the pitch when he suddenly said: 'That's it. If you want the job then you can have it.' He then went on to tell me that the contract would be drawn up and it would be ready for me to sign within the next few days. But he stressed that he wanted the fuss to die down before making the official announcement. I can still remember that there were people up in the executive boxes having their pre-match meals and no doubt looking down at us and wondering what was being said. They would have seen us shake hands and that was the moment the deal was sealed. It was all finalised at that talk and I wondered then and have wondered ever since if any of the people in those boxes realised what was going on right in front of their eyes!

Of course, until it was formalised, I could say nothing. Just as I had had to stay silent over Graeme leaving for Liverpool, now I had to keep quiet about my own future. And still the speculation grew and grew . . .

Even the bookies got in on the act and began offering odds against all the likely candidates. I was not the favourite, though not being a gambler at all, I didn't know too much about all of that until the lads began talking in the dressing-room. Kenny Dalglish, I think, was the front-runner while I was sitting further down the field at something like 7-1. I can remember Mark Hateley coming up to me at training one day to tell me that there was a bookie in England taking bets and he had told his father-in-law to put a few quid on me. The next thing was that all the lads at the park were in on the act – though none of them knew a thing about the chairman's decision to appoint me.

There were some laughs in that brief spell between my knowing and the rest of the world being let in on the secret. One morning at the training ground, Ian Ferguson came up to me and in Fergie's usual direct manner, simply asked: 'Well, are you getting the job or are you no' getting the job?'

So I said to him: 'What do you want to know for?'

And the answer came back: 'You're down to 4-1 and this is the last chance we've got!'

So I told him: 'Well, Fergie, between us, aye . . .'

At that he turned round to signal to a couple of his mates who were watching the training and they disappeared, presumably heading for the local bookies. They stopped the betting eventually. Not that it crossed my mind to have a bet. Not being a gambler, it didn't occur to me. Then later I learned that the bookies would not pay out for three months because they seemed to think that I was only going to be caretaker boss. Nice to have people show that kind of faith in you, isn't it?

There has remained since that time lots of talk and different rumours as to why Graeme left the job. Some people have blamed the SFA for influencing his decision to quit Scottish soccer. That theory became widely accepted because throughout his managerial career Graeme had had stormy relations, to say the least, with the soccer bosses. Others believed that Scottish football was too small a stage for him and that some of the petty attitudes and the jealousies he had to endure had worn him down.

Perhaps there was something to the second suggestion. Graeme did sometimes feel confined by Scottish football. The scene in England is unquestionably bigger, but there is not much we can do about changing that. Graeme had enjoyed his time in the First Division and he knew the challenges that it would throw up at him, and that appealed to him. So, yes, the lure of a bigger, more glamorous stage would have had its appeal.

But you can forget the first theory. Graeme would never have allowed anyone to drive him out of any job without putting up a fight. That would have been totally out of character. He had suffered a lot of frustration in his various brushes with authority and there were times when he was convinced that he was being got at. For example, there was the time when the television cameras caught him standing at the end of the tunnel during a game while he was banned from the touchline. It was not as if he was really breaking the ban, and he certainly wasn't flaunting his presence, because very few people could see him. But the authorities pursued the issue and he was in more trouble, and that was something he felt was almost vindictive, something that need not have been followed up with such seeming enjoyment. That annoyed him. Other similar actions against him annoyed him. But they were never allowed to become major problems. In his more calculating moments, he would never have seen these irritants – and that's all they were to him – as a reason for leaving the country.

In the final analysis, I believe that Graeme simply wanted a change. He was a restless man, never one to put down roots and stay in any one place for a great length of time. Indeed, I would think that his spell at Ibrox was probably as long a time as he had spent anywhere in his career. It just seemed to be in his nature to move on and to keep moving on . . .

He left Spurs when he was just a boy and moved up to Middlesbrough. Then he left there and joined up at Anfield. He was captain of Liverpool when he made up his mind that he was leaving and went to Italy for a spell with Sampdoria before joining Rangers. He always had that wayward quality about him. And, also, there was the emotional pull of Liverpool. He had had his best playing days there and those times, such good times, remember, remained in his mind.

His time at Rangers was not as happy in some ways. Yes, he enjoyed the challenge of building the club and he relished the success he had as a manager. But because of his high profile he was not universally liked, and he knew that. Perhaps he was too big a personality for some of the football people in Scotland; maybe they feared someone like Graeme, who was so much larger than life. But while it might have annoyed him a little, it wasn't a major concern to Graeme.

To be honest, Graeme loved that high profile. He thrived on the publicity. He loved being the biggest name with the biggest club. He came to dominate the back pages – and often the front pages too – in his time as Rangers manager. He was put under the media microscope on an almost daily basis and yet he could live with that. He was almost constantly controversial – and he could live with that, too. I think he enjoyed it. There were times when his faults were exaggerated but he knew that was balanced by the times when his good points were equally exaggerated. None of these things mattered to Graeme in any long-term way. He simply wanted to do the job *his* way, and he did it.

You have to get back to the main point about Graeme's reign at Rangers: he was the man who helped resurrect a great and famous club which had fallen on the hardest of times. As a club, Rangers could always stand up to the examination because of its history and tradition. What Graeme did was to bring the club into the modern football age and transform it. That was done because he had the personality and ambition which enabled him to perform the kind of miracles which few other managers would have been able to accomplish.

Apparently, the most famous of all Rangers managers, Bill Struth, used to be fond of saying, 'Comes the hour, comes the man.' That applied to Rangers in their time of need when Graeme was named as manager. His outrageous self-confidence, some termed it arrogance, rubbed up people from outside the club the wrong way. But the long-suffering supporters saw a manager who was ready to take on the world on Rangers behalf; someone who had the style and belief that the club had lacked for too long.

It was an awkward time when he left, and it became more awkward in the immediate wake of his departure but Graeme can't be blamed for leaving when he did. He did that *his* way, just as he had handled the job itself. At Ibrox we had to carry on because there was still a Championship to be won!

It was something like starting all over again for me. There were just a few games left but instead of trying to qualify for Europe we were now trying to win another title. We went to Paisley, again, for my first match in charge and young Sandy Robertson scored the one goal of the game to give us both points. And then we beat Dundee United at Ibrox and we remained on course for the Championship. Then, before the second-last game of the season, Richard Gough went down with hepatitis and we were struggling to put a team together. That match was at Motherwell and we lost 3–0 while our closest rivals, Aberdeen, stretched their 12-match unbeaten run with a win over St Johnstone which put them at the top of the table.

They were in that position because, although we shared the same number of points and the same goal difference, Aberdeen had scored more goals than we had. And that meant that in the showdown final game of the season when Aberdeen came to play us at Ibrox all they needed was a draw. We had to win.

Now winning at home is not usually a task which is beyond any team. But the defeat at Motherwell had sapped our confidence and our injuries continued to mount and we knew that it would be a scratch team going out to try to take the Championship.

By now I had named my own assistant, Archie Knox, who had joined me, and we knew we were up against it. Poor Archie must have wondered what he had got himself into. He had been at Manchester United preparing for the Cup Winners Cup final against Barcelona in Rotterdam when I spoke to him. Actually, it had never entered my mind that Archie would want to leave Old Trafford and end his long-running partnership with Alex Ferguson. I had sounded out Ray Wilkins to begin with, but he had not wanted to return north. Then in a phone conversation with Archie – we talked all the time – it came out that he would be interested and so I drove down to Carlisle to meet him and talk to him. I outlined the job to him, and he accepted, and then came the difficult job – telling Fergie! To say he didn't like it would be something of an understatement. He broke off diplomatic relations with me for a spell but that situation didn't last. Archie joined up immediately and shared my headaches.

It was a patchwork team we had to put out that day: some of the players who took the field were injured and we collected other injuries during the game. Yet we won, with Mark Hateley scoring twice. The Championship had been won for the third time in succession and I felt a glorious relief. I didn't look on it as my first trophy as a manager. I didn't think I could do that when I was in charge for only the last few games of the season. But I knew deep down that if we had lost against Aberdeen that day then it would have been looked on as the first trophy I had *lost* as a manager.

It was important for me to get that win, important to start off my new career with such an important victory. I don't know how I would have felt if we had lost but, it emphasised for me that as well as having good players around us at Ibrox we had players with a feeling for the club, the type of players who would come through for us in a crisis.

And, of course, we had the Ibrox support that day in full voice. That got to the lads, that lifted them, inspired them, gave them that extra jolt they needed to prove that they could keep on winning trophies no matter what the problems they had had to face over the last three or four weeks of the season.

Graeme phoned me in the manager's office after the game to congratulate me and the players on the victory. When I told him the team that had finished the game that afternoon he wouldn't believe me. We had so many players out of position and yet we held on, we survived, and it gave me the basis for the changes I knew I had to make the following season.

CHAPTER FOUR

Some Changes Had To Be Made

Going into the final games of the season, I knew that the team which might win us a third title in succession was never likely to be the team which would win us a fourth. Even before Graeme's sudden departure, we had discussed together the changes which would have to be made. Now I had to put these into operation myself.

Some of them were necessary because we simply needed new players, fresher players. But mostly they had to be made to prepare us for the UEFA rule changes which had started to bite in earnest the previous season. Quite bluntly, we needed to sign more *Scottish* players. The policy of signing the top players in Britain, which had been used to launch the Rangers revolution, was no longer valid. The limits being placed on 'foreign' players included the English lads who had joined us – in the previous European Cup campaign we had had to leave Mark Hateley in the stand on occasion. The balance of foreign players was working against us in Europe and it had to be turned around.

That summer I moved into transfer action on my own – although it was in the high-spending style of which Graeme would surely have approved. There was nothing new in a close-season spending spree. It had become more or less the norm over the past five years because that was the time to buy new players and we had been constantly building and rebuilding our squad as the seasons passed. We spent a lot of money – but we also brought a lot of money back into the club, which is something that critics of our policy seem to ignore.

Of course, when I had first arrived at Ibrox and we had embarked on the signing policy which was to become a kind of a trademark over the years, we were told that it wasn't possible to buy success. I can't remember how many times I read that in the newspapers. It was not possible to buy your way to the top, Rangers were told from all sides. A couple of years down the line, when the Trophy Room was looking pretty full, the same people were accusing us of buying success – the very thing that they had said was impossible to do. I suppose you just can't please all of the people all of the time . . .

Personally, I don't see that there is any other way now for top clubs to remain at the top without buying quality players. There is always the argument that you should bring on your own young players – and we all try to do that and we have varying degrees of success with youth policies. But when you are with Rangers, and this is a lesson I learned early on, you cannot have a fallow season. You cannot have a year when you don't win anything, a year when you sit back and wait for the talent from your youth team or your reserve team to come through and blossom in time for maybe the next season or the season after that. At the major clubs it doesn't work that way.

At Dundee United the manager, Jim McLean, had the luxury of time. Time to develop the young players he and his scouts unearthed. Time to wait for the

Nareys and the Sturrocks and the Hegartys and the Starks and the Holts and the Milnes and the Goughs to come through the system and mature more or less together. Time after that, after winning a trophy or two, to go back and wait for a further batch of young players to come through and repeat those few years of success.

At Rangers the club cannot stand that kind of patient and persistent policy. Success has to be immediate. Success has to be constant. I've said it often before and I'll repeat it here: Rangers are never more than a couple of games away from a crisis. Two defeats and the world is coming to an end. Losing a trophy means everything has gone wrong and almost everyone has to go. That is the kind of pressure we have to live with. But it's a pressure you grow to accept. It is always there and there is nothing you can do to change it, so what I attempt to do is ignore it and get on with the job at hand.

And if part of that job means spending vast amounts of money on top players then I'll do it. That's why that first foray into the market didn't bother me one little bit. I knew the men I wanted and I knew that they had to be Scots and so I went for them. I bought Andy Goram from Hibs, David Robertson from Aberdeen and Stuart McCall from Everton. The cost was just over £3m but it was cash we had to spend. Trevor Steven left to go to Marseille and we also brought in Alexei Mikhailichenko and Dale Gordon to keep the quality of the squad at a high level. All these new players came to the club at approximately the same time. And, as well as Trevor going, we sold Terry Hurlock and Nigel Spackman. Yet while all these changes were being made and the team was undergoing major surgery, we had to keep winning.

In the early part of that season we found that difficult. We lost in the League Cup semi-final to Hibs and we went out of Europe to Sparta Prague in a tie we should have won. But, by the time we got into the serious part of the Premier League programme, the players had bedded in and we won the title and ended our Scottish Cup jinx run by winning that trophy too.

There was a lot of hard work done behind the scenes that season, adjusting for the new players, making sure that the team did not become too unsettled, and generally trying to make the changes with the minimum of disruption. I think it tells its own story that there was no great comment about the turnover of players that summer. We went through that spell with the minimum of fuss and at the end of the season we still had trophies to keep the support happy . . .

We have continued down the same road because that, in my opinion, is the one and only road for us. We have to make changes every year. The fans want that, they like to see new faces, admire new players and it maintains a high level of interest among them. As well as pleasing the public, the contractual freedom that is now widespread means that you get fewer and fewer one-club players around. Very often you find that players want to move on, and people like John Greig, who spent an entire career with just one club, Rangers, don't really exist anymore. The game has changed dramatically in many ways and that is one of them. At Ibrox we have had to change too, in order that we can keep pace with the developments which occur around Europe.

The first year I arrived at the club we were able to construct a team rather than an entire squad. The second year we found ourselves in much the same position and that is why we ran into problems that season. From the third year onwards I believe we have had a squad of players, a powerful squad, and that is why we have had the run of success which the club has enjoyed.

It was a jolt to my system when I first started handling these huge transfer deals. There was nothing comparable at Dundee United to prepare me for the million-pound signings or the two- or three- or four-million-pound signings that I have made for Rangers. At Tannadice the record signing in my time was Eamon Bannon, who came from Chelsea and cost something like £165,000. And that kind of money was scarcely the norm with Dundee United! In fact, Jim McLean had to sell Raymond Stewart to help finance that deal and leave the club with money to spare. Now, when I was there as Jim's assistant, United were a biggish club – certainly in terms of achievement they were among the leading clubs in Scotland – but going to Rangers pushed me into another football world altogether.

There is an extra pressure which comes when you move into the transfer market because you must make sure that you are buying the right players. You cannot simply splash out money on players without examining every deal very carefully. You have to be sure that the player will fit into your team set-up. You have to be sure that he will improve on what you already have in the first-team squad. And, also, you have to check out the player's background. There is no use bringing someone to the club who might turn out to be a troublemaker off the field. Or, even worse, someone who stirs up bother in the dressing-room. And while you are dabbling in the transfer market you must also have the team winning games – because that is always the bottom line.

As a manager, you are asked to do all these things and you have to remember, too, that the money you are spending is an investment in the future of the club. The money we have spent at Ibrox has been repaid by the vastly increased amounts of cash flowing in through the gates. In the years since Graeme Souness and I took over at Ibrox, the rise in attendances has been remarkable. In our first season we pushed the average gate up to over 20,000. The following season we had moved into the 30,000-plus area, and last season we were up over 40,000. That has been achieved by the results we have had on the field but we have also brought in new players almost every season to stimulate the imagination of the fans. So, for all those who have sniped at the policy which has now been in place for eight years we have thousands more who believe we are doing the right thing.

We have been bringing people back to the game, maybe some people who had stopped going because they were unhappy with the product, maybe others who had not been in the habit of going to games regularly. Whatever, the gates have doubled and every away game is a sell-out as far as our support is concerned. Yes, we are building up our own club – because that is always the primary concern. But we are also raising the profile of the Scottish game as a whole by bringing top players into our domestic League.

Obviously, by doing all of that you encourage sponsors to invest in the club. You also boost the catering at the stadium and all the other commercial aspects of the game which mean the difference between staying solvent and healthy and perhaps losing money and having to lower your sights.

It would be wrong for the club to change the policy now, for several reasons. Firstly, it has been successful for the club, as a look at the Trophy Room over the past few years would show. Secondly, all the major clubs are pursuing the same or similar policies because it is almost universally accepted that this is the road to take. Thirdly, the fans have shown that they want the excitement of watching big-money, star players on a regular basis instead of seeing them on rare occasions only. And, like every other business, football has to give the fans what they want!

Anyone who doubts my theory should take a look at what happened in Italy. Italy is a football-mad country, and yet some years ago the crowds started to decline. The answer found by the clubs was to import the best players from all around the world. The result of that has been to transform Serie A into the best league in the world: the gates have soared, there has been a stampede by every club to import foreign stars and there is a queue of players wanting to go there. And watch what they do with the players. Often they keep a player for a year or two, maybe three years, and then move him on and bring in another fresh face. Foreigners come and go while the basis of every team, the home-grown talent, is less likely to be changed with the same frequency. The clubs keep changing the top players and so there is always a freshness, a sense of constant surprise about things in Serie A. Ultimately, this kind of approach will spread around Europe because it has been shown to be successful. The Italians have demonstrated that. And if they have the best league there is anywhere, then you have to accept that generally they get things right.

It may not always be possible to keep up with the Italians because the financial base for any club in Scotland cannot match the kind of money which is available in Italy. I'm not just talking here about Silvio Berlusconi and AC Milan – I'm referring to any club you care to name in Serie A. In Scotland we are limited by the size of the country, which is an obvious drawback, and also by the amounts of sponsorship cash which are available here compared to what is available in other countries. Look at television money alone and compare the deal that the clubs in Scotland have with the agreement which the English Premiership set up for itself and its member clubs. Italy, Germany, England, France, Spain, even a small country such as the Netherlands can attract more money into the game than is possible in Scotland.

I happen to think that Rangers do magnificently, given the limited nature of the market place in which we operate – but it will never match up to what is on offer in other countries. That is a sad fact of life for the club. We happen to be trapped in a different economy from the clubs we are trying to emulate. There is nothing that can be done to change that fact. It is something we are forced to live with. If you look, even, at the money which is charged for admission in this country you'll find it much less than any of the other countries I have mentioned. We have lower prices than any of the countries we would like to be up alongside. But it is the support we have been given through the turnstiles which has enabled us to maintain a level of spending and continue our challenge to be among the top European clubs.

We were a little bit concerned about how the crowds would stand up after that marvellous, never-to-be-forgotten season in the Champions League, the same season we won the domestic 'treble'. We wondered then if the crowds would hold up the following season – and they did. Indeed, they were even bigger and I think that says so much for the work which has been done at the club. I think the people who follow the club know that we are not going to be standing still. They know that we will always want to progress, that we will always try to maintain the standards which have been set down through the years, or, whenever possible, improve on these standards. No one suggests that is easy but it's something you simply have to take on board when you come to a club of this size. It is part and parcel of being the Rangers manager.

I see myself as accountable to the directors and to the supporters. I have to make sure that the club's money is invested prudently. And I have to make sure that we produce the kind of football the fans want to see from us. They want to see us attacking, going for goals as much as possible, and we try to provide that. It is revealing that Ally McCoist won the Golden Boot as Europe's top league goalscorer two seasons in succession. It is a magnificent achievement as far as Ally is concerned – but it also underlines the team's commitment to attack. I don't want to have it any other way. It's almost a duty to the Ibrox support to entertain them as much as we possibly can.

Changing players on a regular basis can produce its own little worries. As I pointed out before, there are the difficulties of allowing new players to settle in. We have to do that while still trying to win games, and each year that can present problems. At Ibrox, just being able to fit the new men into the basic playing pattern which has been established at the club has become an important part of managing the side. Star players can sometimes bring you headaches because they have their own ideas on how they want to play. You cannot always ask them to do something which is alien to them. When you are handling thoroughbreds then you have to respect their ability and the experience they have picked up. With Dundee United things were more simple in that sense. The players were young, mostly home-grown, and were not, in the early days at least, international players. You told them where to play and they went out to do the job they were told to do. That doesn't work with the more experienced men. You ask players to do what they are good at. That, for instance was always the Liverpool way. I brought in Stuart McCall, and I would never have asked him to try to play the way Ray Wilkins had done for the team.

What we had to do at Ibrox was try to maintain a basic pattern of play, a more or less settled team formation, and then add players to it as and when required. We could not put a squad of players together and simply *hope* for success. We had to put a squad together which would guarantee us success. And once we had that, we had to sustain it. It was no use having slightly good times, or even sporadic success – we had to have players who would keep it all going once we had started the ball rolling. Changes always have to be made. That is something that players as well as fans and managers and directors have to accept these days. Nothing is forever . . .

CHAPTER FIVE

Old Firm Rivalry!

There is no hiding place for any of us when an Old Firm game comes around. That is the one fixture which stands out on its own, set apart from the Cup finals or title-deciders or European Cup games. You can lose any of the others and you will be criticised, but when you lose an Old Firm match then the fans are most often in an unforgiving mood.

And yet it is the one game where you can never forecast the result. I don't care which of us, either Rangers or Celtic, is stronger at the time, form simply does not count. You see more players showing nerves in that fixture than in any other game – and I'm not talking here about young, inexperienced lads; I'm talking about seasoned professionals who have seen everything in the game. Players who have been to the finals of the World Cup. To European finals. To major games in different parts of the world. Yet when it comes to an Old Firm clash – either at our Ibrox Stadium or at Celtic Park – they are a bag of nerves.

I can remember Terry Butcher, for instance, in one of the first games he played against Celtic. He was out there on the park looking absolutely panic stricken. His clearances were being booted into the stand, just thumped away as hard and as far as possible. And I'm talking here about balls that on a normal Saturday he would bring under control before sending off a perfect pass to a team-mate. Now this is a player who normally has a marvellous temperament. Put the big fellow into a Cup final or a major European tie in front of 70,000 fans in, say, Bucharest and he would not bat an eyelid. But the Celtic game got to him, just as it gets to so many of the players.

That's why it can be a manager's nightmare – because players tend to do so many uncharacteristic things, make the kind of mistakes that they haven't made since playing in schoolboy matches. And, as a manager, you sit there on the bench watching all of this and wondering just how much the nerves and the tension and the pressures are going to affect the result. I remember two or three years back we beat Celtic 5–1 at Ibrox and we played so well in that game. The scoreline didn't flatter us in any way. We were honestly that far ahead of Celtic on the day . . .

A couple of months later we travelled across the city to Parkhead, with more or less the same team, and inside half an hour we were three goals down and we could have been even further behind. In that spell Celtic were as far ahead of us as we had been ahead of them in the first meeting. If we had been five goals down at half-time then it would have been a fairly accurate reflection of the play and the chances created. We got our act together after the interval, and while we didn't threaten them very much we were able to keep the score at 3–0. In the build-up to that game we had been clear favourites, because of our current form in the League and because of that earlier result. Neither aspect made the slightest bit of difference on the day. We were given a doing and I could not explain why that happened then any more than I can explain it today. There is absolutely no rhyme nor reason to it.

Similarly, in the season just finished Lou Macari took over as Celtic manager, came to Ibrox on his first day in charge and won the game. By the time of the next fixture, at Celtic Park, Lou had taken his side to a run where they had given away just one goal in nine games. We went into the game without key players, we really had so many of the first-team lads missing, and yet we were three goals up in 20 minutes. We won fairly easily in the end and yet beforehand we had been written off. Like me, Lou would not have been able to give you any reasoned analysis of how that had happened to his team on the day. I mean, Lou had organised the Celtic defence, had got them working in a way that meant they were not losing many goals, and yet before they could get to grips with us they were out of it . . . That's what puts the game in a category of its own. And that's why its appeal will never fade.

I just don't think you can exaggerate the effect the game has on the players involved. There is so much passion, so many emotions are poured into the game that the tension is almost unbearable. Unless you have experienced this at first hand, it's hard to accept just how different these games are from all the others you play. It's almost as if some outside force takes over for the build-up to the game and the match itself. There are times when you feel as if things just move beyond your control. That's why players make mistakes they would not make at other times, why managers get over excited and why the rivalries will never die.

I don't have to be told what it means to the Rangers support. If you have ever walked away from one of those games with the scarf on, celebrating a victory, or walked away with the scarf in your pocket because you have lost, then you don't need to be told the feelings which exist. I know that the fans have to go into their workplace the following Monday and put up with a lot of stick. It happened to me when I went to the games as a fan, and there is never any way that will change in Glasgow. When you lose another game in the League, or even in one of the Cup tournaments, there can be a philosophical acceptance of the defeat. The fans go away disappointed but the general feeling is that they can come back the next week or in the middle of the following week and the team can win and things are OK again. But a bad result in an Old Firm game lasts and lasts and lasts. It lasts until at least the next time you have to play each other. And then if you don't win that one, the hurt goes on . . .

No one has to tell me that. I've been there with them. Either celebrating or suffering. The game is just so different from anything else I have experienced. I can remember Graeme Souness in his first season saying that he would accept losing to Celtic four times in the Premier League as long as he could be guaranteed the Championship. That did not go down well with the Ibrox faithful. I know what Graeme meant: the title is the prize you want and if you win it then everything is OK. But if anyone had asked him at the end of his five-year spell in charge if he still felt the same way then I am certain he would have given a different answer. He would still have wanted the title – but he would also have wanted to beat Celtic. By then he knew that.

When you are involved with Rangers, you have a far different perspective on the Old Firm situation from someone who is involved with Celtic. That's only natural. But, also, I think you have a different outlook from any of the people involved with other clubs. It always gives me a little bit of a laugh when some of these people start to weep crocodile tears over the problems that they believe Celtic have at this moment in time. The game in Scotland, they will tell anyone who will be prepared to listen, needs a strong Celtic. But you have to ask yourself exactly what they mean by that.

Do they mean that they want a strong Celtic team who visit their ground twice a season and beat their team? Or do they mean that they want a strong Celtic who will bring big crowds with them when they visit their ground but they won't be quite strong enough to beat their team?

I don't think that people outside the Old Firm want either a strong Celtic or a strong Rangers. Although they do want the financial rewards that that particular situation can provide for all the other clubs in the Premier League. Or, in all the leagues, come to that. The smaller clubs worry over the decrease in gates when one of the Big Two are going through a bad spell. They worry about the loss of revenue. They don't worry about whether or not Rangers or Celtic are winning games. They'd prefer us both to be losing regularly but, somehow, still be able to subsidise the game by carrying a big travelling support. They don't really want either of us to be in powerful positions because, in the main, they are jealous of the success the two clubs have had over the years and jealous of the support they are able to draw on. I don't think we at Rangers, or Celtic either for that matter, should be kidded that the other clubs care for our plight when things are going badly. That's just so much nonsense!

And as for me, as Rangers' manager, I cannot in all honesty say that the problems Celtic have faced over the past five years or so have concerned me. There is no way that I would say that the game needs a strong Celtic – because I have to concern myself with my own club. We have to set our own stall to be as successful as we can and it does not matter to me what other clubs do. We have our own standards to set, our own successes to chase and it is up to other clubs to get their own acts together. If Celtic, or any other club, raise their standards high enough then they will make a more powerful challenge for the Premier League title than they have in the past. That cannot be something I'd welcome, now can it? My aim each season is to win the Championship. It is not in my interests, nor is it in Rangers' interests, that our traditional rivals get stronger. I don't believe in handing out any mock sympathy. If a fellow professional, a fellow manager, is in trouble then I care about that – but when it comes to Rangers, then they have to be first and foremost in my thoughts. They are all that matters. Others have the job of worrying about the rest of Scottish football.

What I will say is that there is no way that Celtic will stay in their present situation. History tells you that much. Celtic will get out of it, just as Rangers did. But they will do it by their own efforts – just as Rangers did. No one was around offering helping hands when Rangers were in decline, remember. What has been achieved at Ibrox has been achieved by the people who have run this club, the people who have played for this club, and the people who have supported this club over the past eight years.

One of the Celtic directors did observe that there are always periods of decline in any club's history and then the club will climb clear of that. That has happened back and forth across the decades of Old Firm rivalry – first one club and then the other have enjoyed periods of dominance. The only worrying thing for Celtic – and for every club who find themselves in trouble – is that it is becoming harder and harder to fight your way back to the top level.

If you are in decline then you cannot arrest that

decline or correct it by suddenly bringing in 11 youngsters from the club's youth team. That simply doesn't work any longer. That won't bring the kind of success that big clubs and big supports crave nowadays. It is a much more complicated business than it ever was before. The implications of the Taylor Report have raised problems which existed before, perhaps, but which could be shoved to one side to be dealt with at a later date. Now the agenda has been set. Clubs must reach the standards which have been laid down and to do that they must spend money on their stadia. We had our ground more or less in place and up to the exacting standards of the Taylor Report, but we still went out and spent £35m to upgrade the main stand and construct the club deck. Over the whole period of rebuilding Ibrox, we have probably spent more than all the other Scottish clubs combined in upgrading the stadium. Yet we have also been able to fund team-building. Money has been available every season to spend on players.

Celtic are now beginning a major rebuilding programme at Parkhead and their new manager, Tommy Burns, is also trying to build *his* team, as any man who takes over at a club does. But their plight is their concern. I don't say that out of any sense of bitterness, but it remains my point of view that clubs must look after their own affairs. Celtic have to get on with it, as I'm sure they will do, and they'll do so without any sympathy from me and without the over-the-top apparent concern shown by other clubs. All I can say is that it is all a great deal more complicated now than it was even eight years ago when I arrived at Ibrox as the assistant manager!

The one unchanging thing which remains is that the other clubs will always want to beat the Old Firm. Oh, and, of course, we shall always want to beat each other. That's why I tend to ignore all the talk which goes on about how the game needs more competition. How it's bad for the game that Rangers are winning so many of the domestic honours. If it's that bad for the game, then let the other clubs do something about it. Let them raise their standards and provide a better challenge. We would welcome that – but what we would not welcome is a lowering of the standards we have set for ourselves at Ibrox in the period of our success.

Dragging Rangers down to the level of other clubs would not be good for the game. If the others can operate at a higher level then that would be welcomed all round. Scottish football would then be better off. The other season, when we had our unbeaten run in the Champions League and we were able to defeat the English champions Leeds United to reach that stage of the European Cup, I believe that Rangers raised the profile of Scottish football. We were doing it firstly for the club, and that has to be accepted, but we also became standard-bearers for the whole country.

Was that success – we won the treble that season on the domestic front – bad for Scottish football? Was it bad for Scottish football when Celtic were winning nine titles in succession and doing well in Europe? Or when Aberdeen had their run of success at home and abroad under Alex Ferguson – was that bad for the game here? I don't think so. In each case, it was up to the other clubs to mount a challenge more convincingly.

Those clubs, all of them, who tell us that competition should be more exacting should do something about their own situations. Let them try to do what we have done. They have to strive to improve, not wait for us to get weaker.

If that did happen – and I don't believe that it will – there would be no tears shed for Rangers. Not by

Celtic and not by any of the other clubs. It has been like that before and was like that for too long. But no one at Rangers would expect sympathy from anyone at Celtic and I don't think Celtic expect any from us now. We each have to tackle our own problems, get to grips with the worries we all face from time to time and we have to remember that the rivalry between us will never grow less.

This is a one-off situation which does not change if one club is doing well while another is suffering. It's not like that, because, as I've already stressed, this game defies prediction. There are rivalries in other countries, in other great footballing cities, but I don't think any of them contain the passion which envelops an Old Firm game. It stretches far beyond football, with its roots in long-held traditions in the West of Scotland.

The two clubs can never divorce themselves from these traditions. Rangers have a Protestant tradition and that is not going to alter greatly, even though Roman Catholic players have been signed. Similarly, Celtic have a Catholic tradition while they have often played Protestant players. That will never change . . .

We made an effort to change things when we signed Maurice Johnston. It was not an easy decision to make. Graeme Souness and I discussed it and then we went through to talk it over with the chairman. Our decision to try to sign the player was based purely on footballing ability – and that's how it should always be. But we were not naïve enough to think that this signing would not cause shock waves throughout the country. That's why we had lengthy talks before going ahead. We had to wonder how the player himself might react. We had to wonder how our support would react.

What we were not concerned about was how Celtic would react, although we were eventually criticised for signing Maurice after he had apparently agreed to return to Parkhead. But that was their problem. It had nothing to do with us. The player had been to Celtic Park for talks. He had said he would sign and he had posed wearing a Celtic jersey, *but* – and it was a big *but* – he had not signed the forms. Until he did that, he was *not* a Celtic player. I would never dream of parading a player and saying a deal had been done unless the registration form had been signed. Too many things can go wrong. You don't risk that.

We did nothing unethical. We knew the player had not completed the formalities and therefore we were free to approach him. He indicated that he would sign for us and he did so, and *then*, after the deal had been completed, we made our announcement. Celtic were not happy but he had not signed for them and everyone now tends to forget that. We were perfectly entitled to make our move and we did so. The rivalry between the clubs exaggerated what had happened, I suppose. But right was on our side and we got a very good player for the club. The Celtic side of it was their business. It's happened on other occasions when clubs have announced they have signed players when they have not done so. We simply did our homework and we made sure that we signed the player properly.

Maurice handled the situation well. And it never did become as bad as I had feared. Yes, we had objections from some supporters but having been born and brought up in Glasgow I thought these would have been much worse than they turned out to be. The chairman and Graeme were confident they had gauged the reaction about right. What happened was no more than they had expected. The great thing was the attitude taken by Maurice himself. He got on with his job, becoming a very valuable player, and when he started to score goals the fans soon accepted him. He has certainly made it easier for any other player in the future who may want to join Rangers and has the same problems to contend with. But I have to stress that the only way we judged the signing was on ability. And that will always be the case at Ibrox.

CHAPTER SIX

The Learning Process

It was a long and winding road which finally carried me to Ibrox – the stadium which had been at the centre of my football dreams as a schoolboy. Unfortunately, when I was a young player I was never good enough to get the chance to play for Rangers.

As a professional footballer, I was ordinary, very ordinary. And I'm not being the least bit modest when I say that. Over the period I played for Dundee United I like to think that I developed into a good pro, and I did look after my fitness, but in truth I knew that I was never going to be any great shakes as a player.

I was as keen as anyone else when I was a kid. I played for the college team while I was at Coatbridge Tech and at the same time as that I was playing for Chapelhall Youth Club. I was just 15 years old then, a little bit younger than some of the other lads, but because Chapelhall had a few of the other lads from the Tech playing for them, that's where I went. It's the same with everyone, isn't it? You want a game, you want to play and you follow the rest of the lads in your group just to make sure you are playing football somewhere.

It was through going there – and through the lads at college – that I went to play for the Albert Youth Club, which was based in Springburn. The team then was run by a man called Willie Don and recently he was at Ibrox as the guest at a dinner celebrating his 25 years in charge of the club. After playing there I went to Bishopbriggs Amateurs and then I stepped up to the juniors with Ashfield. Three of us went there together – Jim Cameron, Gerry Hernon and me. We were just 17 or 18 and easily the youngest lads playing for Ashfield – but Jim Cameron and I didn't last too long with the juniors. Dundee United saw us and the manager at the time, Jerry Kerr, decided to sign us on the old provisional forms. Actually, Louis Boyle, who ran Ashfield and who was quite a legend in Glasgow junior circles, wanted us to stay for the Scottish Junior Cup . . .

We had joined Ashfield in August and by October we had joined Dundee United but remained playing junior football until the early part of 1967 when Ashfield went out of the Cup. You were allowed to do that then under the old provisional-forms system. I played a few reserve games up at Tannadice when Ashfield allowed me to and continued playing for them until, as I say, the Cup came and went and United called me up to join them, though not as a full-time player – because my father insisted that I finish my apprenticeship before I committed myself to football. Again, that was fairly common. If you had an apprenticeship, then your parents usually wanted you to finish the four or five years necessary so you would have something to fall back on. Fortunately, I've never needed to get the electrician's tools out again. But I did do my stint. I had two years left when I went up to Dundee. Until then, I had worked at the Dalmarnock Power Station for the South of Scotland Electricity Board. United organised a job for me in Dundee and I went to work for a firm called Loudon Brothers up there to complete my five-year apprenticeship.

Initially, I trained at night and worked full time during the day. It was a good club to be at as a young player because Jerry Kerr had always managed to surround himself with a strong core of experienced players. The successes the side had then – and they had some nice results in Europe as well as at home – came from that policy. He added the occasional younger player, and some foreign stars and the mix worked for him.

When I went to Tannadice the Swede Lennart Wing was just finishing his spell there. He was an outstanding player for the club and still there at that time were Tommy Millar, Dougie Smith, Jimmy Briggs, Denis Gillespie and Tommy Neilson – real stalwarts of the period when United won promotion and began to emerge from the shadows of their more famous neighbours, Dundee, across the street. Then they still had a few of their Scandinavian imports, including Finn Dossing, Mogens Berg and Finn Seemann. There was also an influx of experienced Rangers players as I joined up, as players such as Jimmy Millar, Davy Wilson and Wilson Wood all arrived at Tannadice.

I made my début for the first team in a match against Kilmarnock while I was still technically with Ashfield, and so when I moved up to Dundee I felt I had a chance to break through. At the end of that first season – or rather half a season for me – we went to the United States as they tried to promote the game over there. A whole bunch of clubs went over from Scotland and England and played out of different cities. We were based in Dallas, playing as the Dallas Tornadoes, and it was a fantastic experience for me. It allowed me a chance to get to know the players, because as I trained at night I only really saw the full-time lads when I was at Tannadice on match days.

A lot of these older players were good to me back then. Some of the things they taught me I still respect and a lot of what I learned has remained clearly defined in my own philosophy on how this game should be played. Tommy Millar, Jimmy's brother, was a great help to me. So was Denis Gillespie, a greatly under-rated footballer, and Doug Smith, who is, of course, still there. He played longer than any of the others and was just such a good, good professional. Doug is now a director of the club and is also a vice-president of the Scottish League, which is a big appointment for an ex-player to get. Alan Gordon came in from Hibs around then and I soon recognised what Jerry Kerr was after. He liked to have that nucleus of lads who had been around a bit and he allowed them to have their say on how the team was going to play.

Things were different back then and Jerry was probably the last of the old-fashioned managers. I say that in the nicest possible way because Jerry was a remarkable manager for United. Indeed, it's almost impossible to criticise him after what he did for the club. He built the main stand, he took them into the top league and he kept them there during his time as boss. And he took them into Europe, where they beat Barcelona, frightened the life out of Juventus and made United known outside their own country for the first time. But his style of management was from an era which was just dying out as I went to United as a professional.

The age of the tracksuit manager was in its infancy in Scotland and Jerry was completely untouched by it. He ran the club, he picked the team and he bought the players, and then he allowed them to get on with the tactics by themselves. He never took training and he was always in a collar and tie and usually a suit, but in his own way he was successful . . .

To be honest, by this time, Jerry was too set in his ways to ever change. Certainly, he wasn't going to make some kind of dramatic change in the way the club was run. He didn't see any need to, I suppose, and it was hard to argue with him about that. There was no great mystique about the game as far as Jerry was concerned. In fact, there was no mystique at all. He saw it as being down to the 11 players out there on the field, just as it had been in his own days as a player. He also felt that if you had a hard core of seasoned professionals in your side then you wouldn't go too far wrong. Jerry always made sure that he had that.

Nowadays, I am often asked to identify the major difference between then and now. Well, one thing back in those early playing days of mine was that, for the most part, teams were sent out to play the game. You didn't have the players being sent out just to mark someone else out of a match. It might happen on occasions but it never happened in the almost universal way it does now. That kind of negative thinking has damaged the game and brought problems in its wake and it just didn't happen when I was starting out.

It's strange to look back now because, while I was ready to question Jerry Kerr's methods as a young player, I now recognise that Jerry was right for his time and relied on basic tenets of the game to get his teams playing. At the time, though, word was filtering through to all the players that new things were happening. There was a new breed of manager and different tactics and fresh training methods were being introduced around the country. Eddie Turnbull, who was in charge of Aberdeen at the time, was in the vanguard of that movement, and, of course, Jock Stein had worked his own miracles with Celtic. At Tannadice we were untouched by these first seeds of revolution.

Jerry had a different outlook. He was from another generation and he knew that.

Why should he change? He was doing OK and he was putting out teams which had the right blend of players, so why should he suddenly complicate a game which he had always seen as simple? It was an attitude which baffled me at the time, but, in retrospect, it also contained a lot of common sense. When Jerry did talk about tactics – and it was a fairly rare occasion when he discussed strategy with any of the players – he was straight to the point. I can remember once in the dressing-room when he was telling the players what they should do it if they got the ball in the middle of the park. 'Look,' he told them between puffs on that trademark pipe of his, 'when you get possession in the middle just you hit the ball wide and there will always be someone there!' You could not get anything more simple than that. There is no advice which could be more basic, more stripped down to the essentials. That's all he said. And I remember thinking, how will there be someone there? But there was always a player there in a wide position because Jerry insisted that Finn Seemann stick to the right touchline and Davy Wilson hug the left-wing. And it worked. Even in these early days of the tactical explosion which struck the Scottish game at that time, Jerry's way worked.

In later years, as a coach, and now as a manager in my own right, I have thought about that and it has taught me a lesson or two. All Jerry was doing was keeping it simple – and, at the same time, he was making sure that he had the right players in the right positions. Of course, a year or two later the whole change in approach had hit the game and Jerry knew that things had to change – even at Tannadice. He brought in Jim McLean as assistant manager and that was an eye-opener for all of us. Suddenly, we were in

Captain and manager, player and mentor, the two men who have worked so closely together since Richard Gough was a teenage unknown and Walter Smith was running Dundee United's reserve team

Left-back David Robertson was another of Walter Smith's early signings – coming from Aberdeen as Rangers tried to add to their Scots-born players when UEFA's rule on three 'foreigners' only in each team began to bite

Walter Smith says he was just 'an ordinary player' when he was with Dundee United – but here in training he gets to grips with the Ibrox superstar Ally McCoist

Only two this time? Boss Smith holds the Championship trophy and the League Cup after Rangers' 'double' last season

Danish star Brian Laudrup, one of the major summer signings Walter Smith believes will push Rangers on to a new plateau in European football

The four-million-pound man Duncan Ferguson in action against Motherwell – and showing the shooting form which persuaded Rangers to make him the highest-priced player in Britain

Another day, another trophy – this time it's the Premier League Championship Cup after it was presented to Rangers at Ibrox last season.

Crunch time on the touchline as assistant manager Archie Knox attempts to explain to a worried-looking Walter Smith what is going wrong . . .

Goalkeeper Andy Goram may have been placed on the transfer list – but he was quickly taken off again after demonstrating to Boss Smith his desire to stay a Rangers player

Brian Laudrup, the summer signing from Fiorentina, in training alongside Dave McPherson, with Stuart McCall and Basile Boli glimpsed in the background

Striker Ally McCoist gets in his tuppenceworth as Walter Smith gets a point over in training to young Steven Pressley

The manager, and the manager alone, must make all the hard decisions on the playing side, says Walter Smith. That's what he might be doing here

The Greatest Living Ranger – Ally McCoist, a player who survived all the changes which came about with the Ibrox revolution

Flares explode around Rangers fans as their European trip turns into a night of terror

the middle of the whirlwind of change which was sweeping through the game. It had arrived late on Tayside but we had to catch up very quickly and the new man made that clear from the beginning. Now my thinking about the game was stimulated in ways it had never been before. The seeds of my interest in coaching were sown in those early days after wee Jim began to take the training at Tannadice.

Nothing like this had ever happened to any of us at United. The training was far more organised than before. It was also harder and more demanding than it had been in the past. There was a much greater emphasis on fitness when Jim took over and he also began to work on the tactical side of the game. Some of the players, who had maybe become too set in their ways, resisted the changes and were happy just to jog along as they had always done. But all of these new ideas struck a chord with me. I had always been interested in the various developments which were happening in the game. I used to read magazines and newspapers and books by managers which helped to educate me about the game.

I was not a gifted player. Anything I did achieve, and I hit no great heights, came through working hard at the game. But it is a fact that gifted players, naturally talented players, don't always become good coaches. I think that's because ordinary players have to put more work into their game and give it more thought than the lads who find things come easily to them. Exceptionally talented and skilful players tend to find the game easy and so they don't have to worry about the game in the same manner as lesser players do. That's only natural. And to back that view, I have found that as a manager the higher the quality of player you work with the less coaching you have to do. You don't have to work as hard or be as involved with players to the same extent as you do when you are working with younger, less experienced lads. You just don't need the same input as, for instance, I did when I was at Tannadice as coach with Dundee United. It becomes more important to look at a team pattern which maximises the skills of the players. It's important to have a set-up which suits the individuals you have and also might compensate for some deficiencies you might find in certain players in the side.

I find that I'm always more ready to give a player the benefit of the doubt than perhaps Graeme Souness was when he was the manager. When Stuart Munro was with us I felt he developed into a top-class defender but he was not the best passer of the ball and that used to drive Graeme wild. He would just crack up when Stuart sent away a bad pass . . . But, for me, despite his limitations, he was a good defender and therefore still a lad you could use in that left-back position, where he was comfortable. Graeme and I used to disagree on that and, again, I think that underlines how a marvellously talented player can sometimes be too demanding as a manager.

My start on the coaching side came from wee Jim up at Tannadice. When I was 29 I picked up a pelvic injury which hastened the end of my playing career. For about a year or so before that, Jim had had me taking 'S' form youngsters for one night a week, just feeling my way into it, trying to find out how I could adapt to coaching. And, possibly, Jim was taking a look at me to see if I could handle that side of things. When the injury came, I began to do more of the training and I was working with lads such as Davie Dodds, Dave Beaumont, John Reilly, John Clark – the second wave of players Jim had had at Tannadice, those who came just after the likes of Dave Narey and Paul Sturrock and the rest. I enjoyed that and then he asked me if I would like to take the reserve team and be in charge of the side on match days. He also gave me the chance to take the part-time players, who included Maurice Malpas at that time. So, not only had wee Jim sparked my interest when he first arrived at the club, he had now given me the chance to go into the coaching side of the game.

Eventually, he appeared to make up his mind that I was far better doing that than I had ever been playing the game. So, in 1979, he asked me to take over as first-team coach. Until then he had never really had a coach. He had done it all himself with some assistance from the physio Andy Dickson when that was necessary. He had worked that way for seven or eight years by the time he appointed me. It was crazy for him because by then Andy was getting on in years and Jim should have had someone to share the load. I was the one he asked to do that and a couple of years later he named me as his assistant manager. And that was the job I filled until I left to go to Rangers. It was a terrific learning experience for me. Any success I have had as a manager stems from those early days at Tannadice and the lessons I learned then.

As well as working with wee Jim at United, I was lucky enough to get the chance to work with the Scotland youth team. I had started going to the coaching courses at Largs when I was about 25 or so. Craig Brown, Willie McLean and Peter Rice were in charge then and for two years Craig and Willie took the working group that I was in. I took my coaching certificate there and the following year Andy Roxburgh was named national coach and he asked me to join the team of instructors. After that, he asked me to go with the youth team and wee Jim was happy for me to do all this and to gain more experience as I travelled to games with the best young players in the country.

Ally McCoist and Charlie Nicholas were around then, and so I found myself involved with the cream of the youngsters from all the clubs in Scotland – and from some in England, too. It was exciting for me and beneficial. You could see at that level some of the problems that managers have to face when they go into Europe or into World Cups or whatever. It was all there for you – the different approaches you had to take against different countries, the problems you could suddenly be asked to deal with, and the troubles which you can always find when you go abroad to play. It was ideal for me as a young coach to gain that kind of insight and it was satisfying to build up a relationship with some of the players who were starting out on their careers then and who are now among the country's most seasoned and respected professionals. It's been good to have that kind of connection.

But, to get back to wee Jim and his soccer academy at Tannadice – which is what it became. He was one of the most thorough managers you could ever meet. And I mean *anywhere*. I don't care where you go, it would be hard to find anyone who put more into planning for games and for training sessions than he did. That was always one of his great secrets. He would leave nothing to chance. His tactics when going into specific games were worked out to the last detail. And his own discipline and the discipline he imposed on others was very hard to live up to. But he demanded that and he led by example, always.

He insisted that players work in the way he wanted them to. He looked for that from every player in every position. Over the years he worked with tremendous patience and amazing dedication until he got the standard of player he wanted to have at Tannadice. It was then that United began to win trophies and make their mark in Europe and prove how successful his methods could be.

The discipline and the patience he showed during that period impressed me then and has remained in my memory to this day. An awful lot of the players who were with Dundee United then and who stayed with the club for a long period of time had to wait for that success. Wee Jim had to wait for it too and I'm sure that for all of them it tasted that much sweeter when it finally arrived. In contrast to Rangers, he was given time. That was one of the first things which struck me when I came to Ibrox – you don't get time. You have to be successful. And you have to be successful *immediately*!

At a smaller club, these demands are not as great and so Jim built things up gradually. Adding a bit here, then a piece there and then bringing in another ingredient until he had the kind of team he wanted, playing the kind of football he believed in. I know what he went through to produce the success he finally got and because of that he has been a major influence on my thinking and on the way I work.

My backroom staff at Ibrox shows you just how much his methods impressed me. Archie Knox, Davie Dodds, Billy Kirkwood – they were all there at Tannadice and so I know that if I'm not at Ibrox then they will be around to take over the training. This ensures there is a sense of continuity about the place which is always important to players. You don't want to disturb players too much when there is a routine and a certain rhythm about the training. There are times when you want to alter a little thing here or there just to freshen it all up. But the main thrust of training and tactics is always the same and whoever is in charge on any given day has to follow the major guidelines.

When I was at Dundee United and Jim was away from the training ground for one reason or another, I simply picked up on what he had been doing with the players. You knew he had done that on his own for so long that you would really have said that it was impossible for just one man to handle that kind of workload. But he did – and he did it right, too. Gradually, he allowed me to take the training a little more often and as I gained in confidence I would add little bits of my own, maybe some fresh routine I had picked up when I was away with the youth team, or whatever. I'd try it with the reserves first and then I'd let the first team try it and he would give me the OK. That's how our working relationship went. As far as I was concerned, Jim was great to work with. Outsiders don't always believe that when I tell them but, honestly, I didn't have any clashes with him during the years I operated as his number two. I'm still convinced that I could never have had a better training or a better grounding in management than those years I spent working with Jim McLean.

You have to remember that people like me, who did not enjoy any kind of extravagant reputation as players, must carve out a new career when we stop playing. You have to gain a reputation which is separate and quite different from the one you had in your playing days. You have to work hard and gain recognition working in the background. Well, I couldn't have picked a better background to work in or to launch a new career in. Any success that has come to me stems from those times when Jim McLean instilled in me the necessity for hard work and for good habits. His preaching lives on among us at Ibrox because the backroom staff there all went through the same kind of training that I did. Maybe some of them didn't always see eye to eye with wee Jim but they will all pay tribute to his ability as a coach. I doubt if anyone has ever paid proper tribute to the hours that man spent making

Dundee United into the club they finally became. All of us at Ibrox know what he did. He gave all of us that same kind of commitment and I think we're all the same as he was. You put in long hours behind the scenes because that's all you know. It's what you learned.

You have to work out of the spotlight as well as in it. You have work to do with young players, reserves and 'S' form signings. You have to go to watch games, and while the work you do in these situations is largely unseen and unsung, it's vitally important. As well as the willingness to work all hours in all conditions, you also have to be able to use the knowledge you have picked up about the way a club is set up. If you work at the bottom of any business and work your way up, then you get a real idea of how that business is structured. It's the same at a football club, and all of us at Ibrox have seen life down there and understand how a football club ticks over. You have to know about the laundry, about the training kit, about all manner of nuts and bolts which are as essential to the good running of a club as any of the more glamorous jobs you have to do.

I don't need to run around and tell my staff what has to be done. That comes almost instinctively to them now. That's partly because of their Tannadice training – but it's also because I have known them all for so long. Archie Knox has been a pal of mine since we played together – though that's not the reason he is here at Ibrox with me. It helps because you must have a sense of trust in the people you are working with. But you have to look at Archie's background. He was player-manager at Forfar, he was Fergie's assistant at Aberdeen and Manchester United, and he was also manager of Dundee. He learned his trade in the lower reaches of Scottish soccer and then he gained experience of working with international-class players at Aberdeen and Old Trafford.

Davie Dodds was a lad I worked with when I started coaching at Tannadice. He was always a deep thinker about the game and he was also always a Rangers supporter. I knew that from his days in the Dundee United dressing-room. Billy Kirkwood is younger than me by a good ten years but he stripped alongside me at Tannadice and I got to know him well. Again, he was a player who always thought deeply about the tactical side of things.

As you will have gathered, it is no coincidence that all of us were with Dundee United. I think that the biggest pleasure I had in my time as a coach or assistant manager there was in showing that a small, financially limited club could be successful. I was only a part of that, a very small part. I was very proud to be a part of it but it was all down to Jim McLean. He proved that if you work really hard and you build a club on decent foundations, then you can achieve something in the game. That club is a monument to one man. He did it on his own. And he did it his way.

I was fortunate to be involved in the later stages when the players he had signed were coming through, when the players he had spent so many seasons working with were emerging as Scotland internationals. All of that was a testament to Jim and his methods. You have to wonder how many of those Tannadice players would have won the caps they did win without his influence. To be there while that was happening, while League Cups and a title were won and when a tiny team from Tannadice Street reached the semi-finals of the European Cup, was to be part of a very special adventure. And a remarkable learning experience which I shall always treasure.

CHAPTER SEVEN

Growing Up In The Tradition

I must have been just five years old or so when I was taken to my first Rangers game at Ibrox. I think Queen of the South provided the opposition and I do remember that Rangers scored half-a-dozen goals. And that was enough to confirm for me all the stories of Ibrox greatness that I had heard from my grandfather.

It was my grandfather who took me to that game and he had filled my head with stories about the clubs and the players he had seen over the years and the games he had watched. He had been one of the founder members of the Rangers Supporters' Club in Carmyle, where I grew up. That was back in the Thirties, when the club was formed out there.

My father, back when I was young, was more of a man who followed the juniors. He would take me to see the big junior matches, which drew huge crowds at that time, and I'd be watching Cambuslang Rangers and clubs like that. I'd also see Vale of Clyde and Shettleston as well but when it came to senior matches my grandfather was the person who took me to watch Rangers. His favourite player was Willie Waddell, and he used to talk about him and about the other top players who had been in various Rangers teams.

He used to tell me stories about how he would walk from Rutherglen into Glasgow to catch the train up to Aberdeen to follow the team, walk to and from the game at Pittodrie, and then get back to Glasgow and walk all the way out to Rutherglen again. And always these stories would be laced with the names of players, the results of famous games and a list of the cups and the titles he had seen Rangers win. So he would take me to the games until I was old enough to go on my own, and that was when people like Eric Caldow were in the team and Jimmy Millar, who was always a favourite of mine and who I played with up at Tannadice eventually, was also in the side.

That was the kind of atmosphere in which I grew up. It was football, football, football, with my father talking about the juniors and my grandfather talking about Rangers, and I just sat there listening to all the stories and dreaming of maybe being able to play for the club . . . That was the dream of all of us in the village, though not just to play for Rangers because there were other lads in the village who wanted to play for Celtic. It was split almost down the middle. There was one lad who lived two doors down from me who wanted to play for Partick Thistle, I can remember. And there was another lad who supported Clyde, but in the main the split was an Old Firm one and that's the way it is today too. It doesn't change.

From the start I think I realised the size of the club. Just going to Ibrox was such an occasion when I was a youngster: the crowds were amazing and the players were our heroes. And the legends from the past crowded into your mind because they were there in your grandfather's memory. It is through all of that, through the stories which are handed down, through the personal memories you collect yourself that the tradition of the club is recognised by all the supporters.

Tradition is important to all of us at Ibrox. I know there are those people who say that you cannot operate on history, that you cannot live in the past and all of that. But that is not a view I would agree with. When you have a club with a rich tradition, then you examine that tradition and take from it what can still remain important to the club in any era. It is something which is almost tangible whenever you walk into that Ibrox foyer. You live with these feelings every day of your life and you can learn from the club's history. Certainly, things have got to move on. No one is suggesting that you stand still and ignore modern methods or modern thought. Attitudes today differ from those prevalent 20 years ago, never mind 120 years ago. But tradition, the kind of tradition which has helped shape Rangers, will always have its value. You cannot avoid tradition at this club. Nor, when you become a part of the club, do you want to avoid it . . .

Every single thing that happens at the club is related to something that happened here before. There is always someone around the place who will remind you of that. Or there will be someone who says: 'Old Bill [*the legendary manager, Bill Struth*] wouldn't have done that . . .', or 'Deedle [*another former manager, Willie Waddell*] would do it this way'. You listen to all of that and you take on board what you feel still applies to the present day. After all, managing a club today is a lot different from doing the job 50 years ago or even 20 years ago. The media focus is so much greater now than it ever was then.

There has always been a tradition at Ibrox, for example, that players report for training with a collar and tie – and despite recent objections to this, that's the way it will stay! Sure, it's a little strange when you first arrive from another club to find that rule in place. But if you think about it, maybe that's why it was there in the first place – to remind each and every player that this is not just any club. This club is different. This is Rangers Football Club. And it works because the players *do* wear collar and tie and they understand why that is being done. It's another small way in which the club was set apart from other clubs in Scotland when the traditions were first being born.

On match days we insist on club blazers and flannels. There seemed to be a period when that was not enforced, but Graeme Souness and I brought it back. I still have memories of seeing the Rangers players when I was still at school, and they were always wearing the blue blazers with a huge badge on the pocket and the braid round it on match days. It's something which set them apart from ordinary people and from other footballers. So we decided to restore that discipline and now the players must wear the club uniform on match days – home and away. We relax the dress code when we are travelling abroad and the lads are allowed to wear leisure-suits or tracksuits. When something which has been a part of the club's heritage is still able to be applied in the present day then why shouldn't that be done? There are clubs who envy us our tradition and I believe it is something which must be cherished.

I suppose that's why I decided to put up photographs of all the former managers on the wall of my office. At some clubs that would have taken up all the available space – but it's not that way at Rangers. I am just the ninth manager in the club's 121-year history. The others are, in order: William Wilton, Bill Struth, Scot Symon, Davie White, Willie Waddell, Jock Wallace, John Greig, Jock Wallace again, Graeme Souness and then myself. Some clubs have had as many managers as that in ten years!

Anyhow, they are all hanging there in the office.

A huge slice of history looking down on me. It helps to keep me conscious of the history of the club. Whenever you start kicking a ball around and hearing the stories of Rangers you begin to know what this club has been about, but it's always nice to have the little reminders around. The board room has pictures of all the club chairmen around the walls and so I thought it was appropriate for the managers to have the same kind of 'gallery'. I knew that the pictures of the various men who had managed the club were scattered throughout the stadium and so I had them gathered together. After all, they were the men who moulded the club. William Wilton was there at the very beginning and then you had Bill Struth, who started in my grandfather's time and who is the father of the club as it is today. And Scot Symon, the last of the old-fashioned 'gentleman' managers, and Willie Waddell, who brought the European Cup Winners Cup to Ibrox. They are all up there, reminding me of what has gone before. It's interesting to note, too, that there have been more chairmen than managers! How many clubs around could say the same?

When we won six titles in a row it was a pretty remarkable achievement and one which had never been done before by the club. Five successive Championships was the record before. But while it is something you can take pride in, you then look at some of the other achievements of the men who are watching over you and you realise just what this club has always been about.

Bill Struth won 18 League Championship trophies. Now, you know right away that the likelihood of that being matched in modern times is not too great. You realise just what a superb feat that was – 18 times he guided the team to a title. It's extraordinary. The other managers, too, had their moments, their victories and their own little pieces of history. I don't think it does you any harm if, now and again, you look at these pictures and remind yourself of what was done here at this club long before you were ever involved. There's always that little reminder that no matter how well you think you are doing there were a lot of people who maybe did better in their time in charge.

Sometimes traditions have to be adjusted a little to fit in with modern times but that doesn't mean that they should be forgotten. As long as I am manager of Rangers, the basic traditions which have made this club such a dominant force in Scottish football since the game began will stay in place. Times change, the demands may be greater than they were and certainly the media hype has increased enormously – but none of these things will change the way Rangers go about their business and have always gone about their business.

Over the years, we have had our troubles with the media – but, mainly, these arrived early in my time with the club. For the first two or three years we suffered some horrendous publicity. Controversy just seemed to follow us around. It seemed to haunt us. Often our reaction to criticism or bad publicity was spontaneous and that led to confrontation, which none of us wanted but which we couldn't walk away from. If we had had more experience, things would have been handled differently and I'm sure Graeme would agree with me on that if anyone asked him. We get these problems because of the interest which surrounds the club. Every little incident becomes a major issue. Every minor row becomes front-page news. You cannot escape that. It is just something you have to take on board when you come to Ibrox. You have to learn how to handle it. But I often wonder how Bill Struth would have dealt with the demands of the modern media. Winning all those titles might have been easier!

CHAPTER EIGHT

The Roll Of Honour

Technically, the first trophy I won was the title in 1991 – but it's not a victory campaign which I can take much credit for. I'd been in the manager's job for only a few weeks when we clinched that one shortly after Graeme Souness had gone to Liverpool. Mind you, I was fairly clear in my own mind that day when we faced Aberdeen that if the game was lost – and the Championship with it – then I would carry the can. I was also conscious that if we won the Championship much of the credit would go to Graeme for putting us in the right position. It was a bit of a catch-22 as far as I was concerned, and what I had to do was push any personal thoughts to the back of my mind and think only of the team and what another win meant.

It was only when it was over that I felt a great sense of relief, because it had been my first major test as a manager. Sure, I'd had loads of experience and this was Rangers' *fourth* Championship in my time at the club and the *third* in a row. But it was the *first* that I had achieved on my own. I think it was important to prove to people that I could handle that type of situation and, to some extent, I had to prove it to myself. Going into the game against Aberdeen in the decider – and it was a last-match decider – I felt more nervous than I have ever felt before. But the players went out, patched up as they were, and won the game decisively and we were on our way – though we did have a hiccup to come early in the next season.

The League Cup was the first trophy I was asked to defend. It was a tournament which had been good to us. In the years since I arrived at Ibrox we had been winners four times in five years and beaten finalists in the other season, the only one we had missed out on. This time it was different – no victory, not even an appearance in the final, and the setback was a personal blow for me.

We lost 1–0 to Hibs in a Hampden semi-final and the Edinburgh side went on to beat Dunfermline 2–0 in the final. The goal which knocked us out of a tournament which had been seen almost as our personal property was scored by Keith Wright. That was bad enough, but it was a mistake from Andy Goram against his old club which brought about the defeat. And Andy had been one of my first summer signings. That night was a lesson for both of us. Andy learned very quickly the demands made on players at Ibrox – and he took that lesson to heart!

I learned that management is a difficult game and there was a brief period then when I questioned my own credentials. I was looking at myself to see where I might have made errors. We had gone out of Europe to Sparta Prague as well and there was that little bit of pressure and a feeling that questions were being asked about me. About my judgment in buying players and about my methods of handling the team. That was only natural, I suppose, but it was not the best of times for me. Fortunately, these times, these good times, lay not too far ahead . . . The defeat against Hibs was to be the only one we suffered in a domestic Cup competition for two-and-a-half long years. And as well as that glittering success at home, we were also to cram in the Champions League run which gave us an undefeated season in the European Cup. The early setback worked in our favour. To some extent the defeats against Sparta and Hibs came as the new players I had bought were still finding their feet. They were still learning what it takes to be a Rangers player and about the unceasing demands for success that are made at Ibrox. At their other clubs a League Cup semi-final could be hailed as some kind of success. At Rangers anything short of winning a trophy is failure. The new lads learned fast and from that semi-final defeat onwards the club went off on its most successful run ever.

In an unbelievable spell we set record after record for the next three seasons. We ended our Scottish Cup jinx – it had lasted an incredible 11 years – that season and took the title again. The next season we won the Championship for the *fifth* successive time and won the treble, as well as staying unbeaten in the European Cup. Then last season we won our *sixth* title in a row, a new club record, and missed out on the treble when Dundee United defeated us in the Scottish Cup final. In those three seasons we competed for nine domestic trophies and we won *seven* of them. And those magnificent seven were won in a consecutive sequence which lasted for two whole years.

Even in the Rangers history books there has not been a run to equal that and the most satisfying thing for me about it all – apart from the very obvious delight at winning the trophies – was the reaction of the players. Almost to a man, they claimed in that period they had played the best football of their entire careers. Now I'm talking here about experienced lads, such as Mark Hateley who has been all over Europe in his time as a player. But that spell was his best. Other players said the same. And they kept on that high for more than the two years. From that defeat against Hibs they picked themselves up and set out on the run which was to bring us all so much satisfaction.

Winning is essential to any manager, especially a Rangers manager, but the most rewarding thing was knowing that I had been able to bring so many players to their peak for these challenges. That's where you feel most satisfaction as a manager, just knowing that you have been able to do your job in the best way possible. That you have won the trophies you have gone after – and you have brought the best out of the group of players you had at your disposal. You simply cannot ask for any more than that.

We all pushed ourselves into the history books and here is how some of that history was made . . .

19 April 1992 – Rangers 4 St Mirren 0
This was the first trophy win for the group of players I had brought together. Hearts had been our main challengers that season but this match, against St Mirren at Ibrox, gave us our fourth successive title win. It was a day of real celebration for the new players in particular. Lads such as Andy Goram, David Robertson and Stuart McCall had joined us looking for this kind of glory. They had been bitterly disappointed at losing in the League Cup – falling at the very first hurdle, so to speak, but this made up for it.

Coisty (who else?) gave us the lead in 20 minutes or so. Then in the second half we had goals from Gary Stevens, Coisty again and Pieter Huistra to take the title with some style as more than 40,000 fans celebrated.

We celebrated, too, especially those lads who were getting their first medals . . . and there was more to come. Much more, because by now we had qualified for a Scottish Cup final appearance and that was coming in a month's time . . .

10 May 1992 – Airdrie 1 Rangers 2
This was a nervous day, a build-up during which we were reminded from all sides that Rangers were jinxed in the competition. That is not the kind of thing I normally pay any attention to – but once the Championship had been won then we heard little else. Since arriving at Rangers, I had only been involved in one Scottish Cup final and several embarrassing early-round defeats. The solitary final was against Celtic and we had lost 1–0 to a Joe Miller goal in 1989. This was the first chance we had had since then of lifting the Cup. To counter the nerves, there had been a feeling that this just might be our year after the semi-final at Hampden. It was an Old Firm clash, that most volatile and unpredictable of games, and we had David Robertson ordered off after just six minutes for fouling Joe Miller. But, as usual on these big occasions, you can look to Coisty for something special. He delivered. A goal just before half-time from the man himself gave us victory and a return visit to Hampden to face Airdrie.

Going into that game we had just one player with a winner's medal – David Robertson, who had been with Aberdeen when they won the Cup two years earlier. The burden of recent history lay heavily on the others, and, while we were clear favourites against the men from Broomfield, we knew they had reached a League Cup semi-final spot that season, just as we had and lost out in controversial and unfortunate circumstances. In this tournament, after a couple of easy games to play their way in, they had beaten Hibs and then Hearts in the quarter-finals and semi-finals. It was never going to be easy.

I remember thinking that this was a game where we had to score first. A goal, particularly one which pushed us in front, was what we needed to calm our players and our fans. It worked out that way for us. David Robertson made an opening and Mark Hateley scored after half an hour, and then, just on the interval, Coisty struck for the 39th time that season. We went in two goals in front and while Airdrie scored through Andy Smith near the end and caused us some worrying moments in those closing minutes we held on, took the Scottish Cup, ended all talk of a jinx and completed our first League and Cup double for 14 years. It was a nice end to my first full season as manager. And that win helped wipe out the memory of defeat by Hibs at the same ground six months earlier!

25 October 1992 – Rangers 2 Aberdeen 1, after extra time

This was a win which underlined the determination of these players of mine. We went into the match after meeting Leeds United in a European Cup tie in the previous midweek. That had been a gruelling, physically demanding game at Ibrox, and, while we had a victory to build on, I knew it had taken its toll on the team.

This was the fourth time in six years we had met Aberdeen in the League Cup final and they were the one team in the country who had beaten us at the last stage of the tournament. They were clearly going to be fresher than us – but the steely approach that was to impress so many people in Europe later that same season was demonstrated magnificently.

We might have gone in front very early when Ian Ferguson hit the post, but the goal did arrive and it was an early one. Stuart McCall scored in the 14th minute after their goalkeeper, Theo Snelders, had been caught out by the recently introduced pass-back rule. He tried to chest away a ball which had reached him via defender David Winnie. It broke to Stuart, who scored, and it remained that way until halfway through the second half, when Duncan Shearer equalised.

That pushed the game into extra time and the worry for us was how the players would be able to cope with that after their midweek efforts. They dominated that period, just as they had controlled most of the game, and our pressure paid off when Gary Smith sent the ball through his own goal while menaced by Mark Hateley. That was enough to give us the Cup and put it back in the Trophy Room at Ibrox, which had had a strange look without it.

2 May 1993 – Airdrie 0 Rangers 1

It was Aberdeen who provided the main thrust of the League challenge to us in this season – just as they did in the two Cup competitions. They finished runners-up in all three, but that's getting ahead of myself.

This was the game which confirmed us as champions and put us in the Ibrox record books. I didn't know that would be the case beforehand but after the game at Broomfield the chairman was quick to point out to me that we had equalled the best-ever Rangers performance of five titles in a row.

It was perhaps not our best performance of the season, but by now Ally McCoist was out with his broken leg and it was his deputy, Gary McSwegan, who grabbed the goal which gave us victory. That strike came in 46 minutes in a game where we found goals difficult to come by – and remember we scored an amazing 97 goals in our 44 League games that season. But that single goal was enough to confirm us as champions. And we were left to look forward to the Scottish Cup, the lure of the 'treble' and the culmination of one of the finest seasons any club will ever know.

Aberdeen now stood between us and our last little piece of glory in a tournament which had not always been good to us. But we had the memory of victory the previous season and the thought of the 'treble' lifted everyone on the staff.

29 May 1993 – Aberdeen 1 Rangers 2

We had not had it all that easy in the 1993-94 Scottish Cup – we didn't get one home draw. Mind you, after the first game, at Motherwell, we went down the Leagues to play Ayr United and Arbroath before we faced Hearts in a semi-final at Celtic Park. We beat them 2–1, even though we had gone behind to an Alan Preston goal after an hour. Dave McPherson equalised for us, Coisty nipped the winner and we were through to meet Aberdeen, again at Celtic Park because of rebuilding at Hampden.

The Pittodrie team had snapped at our heels in the League race, forced us into extra time in the League Cup final and had clung on determinedly to be there waiting for us in the final. We were, of course, without McCoist and that called for some team adjustments to be made. I played Ian Durrant just off Mark Hateley, used Pieter Huistra wide and had young Neil Murray in midfield. And it was Neil who put us ahead with a fierce long-range drive after 22 minutes. Mark Hateley slammed in a second and it was not until the last quarter of an hour that Aberdeen worried us seriously. That came when Lee Richardson scored their goal but, again, we held on and the 'treble' was completed.

It was a superb feeling knowing that we had won all three domestic honours, and you have to remember that while we were doing that we were having that superb European Cup run. We beat Danish champions

Lyngby then Leeds, and in the Champions League the champions of Russia, Belgium and France were not able to defeat us. That still gives me a warm feeling . . .

But, at Rangers, as I have constantly stressed, there is no time to sit back and count your medals. The game goes on, the trophies are waiting to be won and you are expected to win them. In almost no time at all we were back in another League Cup final and on the trail of another domestic hat-trick . . .

24 October 1993 – Hibs 1 Rangers 2
This was the sixth successive domestic trophy we were after – and we went into the final against the last team to have beaten us in a Cup competition in Scotland, Hibs. Two years before they had knocked us out of this competition in the semi-final. Now they stood between us and another Cup win.

We had had to beat Aberdeen in the quarter-finals when we finished up 2–1 winners after extra time. Then we beat Celtic in the semi-finals – with the match being played at Ibrox. We had Pieter Huistra sent off but were still able to win 1–0 with a Hateley goal and so it was on to Hibs and another final at Celtic Park. We went in front when Durranty scored but an own goal from Dave McPherson brought Hibs back into the game. It needed something special after that to break the deadlock. And I had put that ingredient on to the bench just in case. Ally McCoist was just coming back from injury and had played two full games and made another appearance as a sub. He was a substitute again because I didn't know if he would have been able to last the full 90 minutes. I made up my mind that the game needed him and on he went with 20 minutes left to play. And nine minutes before the end he scored with a spectacular overhead kick. Only McCoist could have done that – and I said that to him after the game. It had

been a gamble to have him involved but the one thing
you are always sure of with him is that he can sniff out
goals better than anyone. He has a knack for that. It's
why he was Europe's top League goalscorer and
winner of the Golden Boot two years in succession.
And it's why he has been so valuable as a player to
Rangers and Scotland.

But that strike beggared belief: it was conjured out
of nothing, it was one of his finest goals for the club and
it kept us on our winning run . . .

4 May 1994 – Hibs 1 Rangers 0
The scoreline isn't one that I want to remember – and
there was no lap of honour from the players at Easter
Road after this match. But winning the Championship
this season, our sixth in succession, gave me more
satisfaction than any of the other trophy wins we have
had. This was a long, hard slog for the players.

Motherwell lost that night, too, and that meant we
had won the title, ending a period which had drained
the players tremendously. When you look back you
don't see any team which has been able to win back-to-
back trebles. We came within a goal of doing that when
we met Dundee United in the Scottish Cup final. But
we did win the League again despite a crippling series
of injuries which would have crushed lesser teams.
Andy Goram was out for most of the season. So was
Ally McCoist. And Ian Durrant. The team was chopped
and changed, and yet the players delivered.

It's hard to tell just how much they had been
drained by the efforts of the previous season. Certainly,
there were stress injuries which affected us during the
season. And mentally there must have been a
tremendous strain. This was our seventh domestic
honour – a demanding run which no other club had
ever achieved. The constant pressure, the never-ending

demand for success must have taken its toll. I'm not trying to make any excuses here. I don't think I have to make excuses for players whose names will go down in history. I'm simply pointing out the kind of pressures which they went through.

There was no time for them to relax. No time for them to sit back and say 'haven't we done well' – it was on to the next game, the next competition, the next challenge. For them to have kept themselves up for such a period of time was incredible. For them to have taken the title once more, after all the early season problems and the lingering worries which hit us, was amazing.

You won't find me criticising them because, at times, they didn't show the same style as they had the previous season. Winning last year asked for different qualities from the players. It wasn't just about their footballing ability, it was also about the physical and emotional reserves they had left to draw on. It was to their eternal credit that they were not found wanting in the toughest competition of them all – the Premier League Championship. That is always the most difficult prize to win and always the one you want to win most.

We may have been criticised but we won it again and we remained on course to challenge Celtic's record sequence of nine wins.

It's that record the fans keep talking about. I'd be wrong to tell you that we don't think about it at the club. It's there in the record books and it remains a challenge. When you have won three or even four then it seems far off. When you have won six it is tantalisingly close. But you also realise, as a manager, just how great a feat that was.

What we have to do, however, is try to win the next title. Look at this in the short term and then we get that bit closer each year. As a fan, I think it would be fabulous to do it. To equal it. Or to go one better. I mean, every victory over Celtic, our oldest rivals, is a cause for some celebration, so if you can equal that record or beat it then it would be a massive boost to the club.

But, as a manager, I know how hard it is. We took some stick in the first season or two when our players were dubbed mercenaries – mainly after we had lost the title in the second year. Now no one says that any longer because the players we have brought to Rangers have proved that they are ready to take on the traditions of the club and they have taken on board the fact that they *must* be successful. And they have been, more successful than any team which has gone before them. If we were to beat the Celtic record it would be another tremendous achievement for them. It's something we would all want but it's something that we realise we all have to work hard to get.

CHAPTER NINE

A Greek Tragedy – And Beyond!

A great deal has been made of our relatively poor European record over the eight years I have been with the club. And, it's true that apart from a couple of occasions, we have not been convincing in the UEFA Cup or the European Cup.

Of course we have come up against powerful teams in some of the early rounds of these competitions. Red Star Belgrade won the European Cup after knocking us out. And Sparta Prague went on to defeat Marseille and reach the first of the Champions' League formations. We had our greatest run when we got to that stage ourselves. But, over the past two seasons, we have failed to get there again. Levski Sofia and then AEK Athens knocked us out and a great deal of hysteria surrounded the most recent of these disappointing results.

I'm not making any excuses here. I said after the first game in Athens that I tried the wrong defensive tactics for the game – and in the first half they didn't work. But there were other reasons, too, for our failure and in the future I believe we are going to find it more and more difficult to reach the so-lucrative Champions' League.

There is no way I can see – unless we win the European Cup itself – that the champions of Scotland will gain automatic entry to the League set-up. The complex seeding system which is now being used appears to be biased in favour of the wealthier countries. There's no doubt in my mind that the most powerful nations will *always* be invited to the League format. The champions of Italy and Germany and Spain and England and Holland will inevitably find themselves there without the dangers of facing a preliminary round game which can always be tricky.

Now after our appearance in the Champions' League when we went *ten* games undefeated in the tournament and were just pipped by the winners, Marseille, for a place in the final, we lost ground in the seedings.

Don't ask me how that happened. I don't know. I haven't a clue in fact. And no one was able to explain that to me satisfactorily. Nor is it easy to understand how Manchester United strolled into the Champions' League last time round when *no* English club has ever qualified for that part of the tournament. But while we were losing to AEK, United were able to sit back and relax knowing that they had earned £1.2 million simply by being asked to join the very lucrative party.

In the years when the English champions and the German champions didn't go through there was a lot of anguish around UEFA headquarters in Switzerland. Quite simply the sponsors who pour huge amounts of money into the European Cup were not happy that two huge markets were not going to be represented. Similarly the television companies didn't like it either. We were in it that year but Scotland will never generate the size of audience that other bigger countries do. That is a fact of life that we have to live with. We are trapped in an economy which just cannot match that of other major players in the European game.

There is nothing we can do to change that. Rangers, as a club, have resources which will match most of the clubs from around Europe, with the obvious exception of the Italians. We have a state of the art stadium. We attract huge crowds to *all* our games, not just the glamour European clashes. But the market place for the sponsors and the television people isn't one which will match the big nations on the Continent or even the one which exists across the border in England.

We all know how important it can be to any club to reach the Champions' League. The money earned can be as much as five million pounds. But more important, you are maintaining the status of the club. And country. All the time, too, you are able to give the supporters what they want, the opportunity to see the top teams in Europe playing at your ground. The real problem is that *every* club who plays in the preliminary rounds realises the rewards which are available. They want to be there as much as you do.

When you draw a team with undoubted ability then you can find yourself in trouble, especially as we are being asked to play the matches so early. Our first tie in Athens came before the season at home had kicked off properly. I watched AEK. Archie Knox watched AEK. Both of us agreed that they were more difficult opponents than Levski had been. They were also better than Sparta Prague had been and these were the two sides who knocked us out in previous seasons.

Remember, there are fewer and fewer 'easy' teams scattered around Europe nowadays. Aberdeen found that out when they lost to Skonta Riga from Latvia. In the European Cup, though, it is cut down even more because only 24 teams are eligible. The champions of most of the lesser football nations are now relegated to playing in the UEFA Cup.

The horror story for Scotland would be if that happened to us in the future. At the moment we are sitting close to the top eight seeded nations but a preliminary round defeat will do nothing to help us. It's something that all of us are deeply conscious of and something we are desperate to improve on in the future. We have to do better in Europe if we are to be able to remain in the European Cup competition – if we slip out of the top 24 it would be disastrous for the whole of Scotland.

On a personal level, I have found it hard to accept that in Europe there have been times when we have known less success than I did with Dundee United when I was there. The draws have been less kind but possibly it's also that the demands on us have been heavier.

Whatever, we know that as a club we *must* do better. If we had qualified for the Champions' League this time round then the summer spending would have been wiped out immediately. That is how you have to assess what qualification means to you in a financial sense. We spent that money in a bid to make an impact on Europe but we were out before Brian Laudrup and Basile Boli had had time to get to know their new team-mates.

If we are to avoid the unthinkable – the Scottish champions excluded from the top European tournament – then we have to give the domestic game an overhaul. I don't mean by that that we should start tinkering around with the Leagues again. Or changing a little bit here and another little bit there just hoping against hope that we are going to finish up with the right set-up. We need more than that. We were lumbered for three years with a massive and exhausting 44-game Premier League programme.

Forty-four games – think about that number of matches! Then you add League Cup games and Scottish Cup games and European games and international games and then questions are asked when our teams don't sail through their European games with victory after victory.

The players are being asked to do too much. It is as simple as that. At a club like Rangers the burdens are heavier because we have been enjoying a period of success which saw us in League Cup finals and Scottish Cup finals as well as playing in the Champions' League for one season. We also have a fair number of international players. So you finish up with lads being asked to play 60 and 70 games a season and you discover that you cannot ask them to train too much during the week. It's impossible to do so. You are actually trying to find things for them *not* to do, to get some break away from training because the playing part of it has been so severe. Asking players to do too much eventually damages them. It leads to more and more stress injuries and it also damages them mentally. You have to try to avoid a staleness creeping in and it's not easy to do that. Right now we have very little time available to spend with the players in improving their skills. It's a little better now because of the change in the League programme. Thirty-six games is much easier to handle but we still have too many matches.

I can remember Alex Ferguson, the Manchester United manager, saying to me that he was thinking about playing a reserve team in the Coca Cola Cup to allow his first team players a chance to stay fresh for Europe. I know exactly what Alex means.

The League Cup or Coca Cola Cup is given too much importance in Scotland and in England. The winner gets a place in the UEFA Cup for example – and I simply cannot agree with that logic.

The League is a test for any team. It is the tournament which rewards consistency and I strongly believe that apart from the Cup Winners Cup, where entry is gained by winning your own domestic Cup competition, all other European places should go to the clubs who do well in the League. It is the fairest way and it makes sense to me that results based on a whole season – rather than putting together four results at the start of the season – should be recognised.

I know that in many European countries the Cup itself is not rated as being very important – but there is something special about that for me and for people in Britain. The fans like the Cup. When it comes around early in the New Year they look forward to it . . . but the League Cup is not something with the same tradition. If I had my way then I'd be happy to see it scrapped completely and some more fixtures cut from the list!

There is really a catastrophic situation over the number of games played in Britain. No other country takes on board the same workload we do here. When you are playing Saturday-Wednesday-Saturday for several seasons without a break then something has got to give. Usually that something is the players' fitness. You then get a situation where the player is playing matches when he is not 100 per cent fit physically or mentally – but he has to go on with the grind. It's the major clubs who suffer. You play ten months of the year, maybe play international games in another month, take three weeks off and start all over again . . . it's a recipe for disaster.

The only time the authorities pay any attention to the needs of the bigger clubs and the players is when there is some kind of breakaway threat. That alerts them, they make some changes and then hope everything will settle down again. Basically the bigger clubs remain voices in the wilderness as far as the game in general is concerned. The smaller teams still rule things and they either don't care about our problems, or don't recognise that they even exist. But soon there will have to be a re-think and perhaps even a major re-structuring of the game if we are all going to survive.

The overcrowded fixture list isn't just hurting the Premier League clubs, it's also affecting the international team. When did you ever think that Rangers playing Dumbarton or Alloa would be able to draw a bigger gate than Scotland facing Italy in a World Cup game? But that happened the other season. An international match is now becoming just another match now – another game in a seemingly never-ending sea of fixtures. That can't be right. But, for the moment, it is a fact that clubs are taking over from the country in terms of major interest. The move to having international games on a Saturday is going to help. It will take away the need for those extra midweek fixtures which clutter up the season and make the job of the players that much harder.

Club managers have been preaching this message for years – that the number of games should be decreased and that players should have fewer matches in midweek. That allows time for all of us to work with the players – and also gives them recovery time between games. Time to have injuries treated, time to rest if that is what is necessary, time to hone their skills and work on any part of their game which needs developed.

Over the three seasons I have been Rangers' manager there has been no time for that. All we have been able to do with the players is try to keep up their fitness level during the season and try to allow them time to shake off the nagging injuries which come with the general wear and tear that these heavy domestic programmes bring in their wake.

During the Champions' League run we had to resort to taking the players for a walk and finishing up in a transport cafe for coffee and bacon rolls because to work them any more would have been counter-productive. But is that really what we want to be doing? Of course not – but the system left us with little alternative. We have eight games fewer now but there are international games almost every month in the European Championship qualifying section and that, too, will takes its toll.

Some real change has to come otherwise we will drift lower and lower in the European ratings and I have already spelled out the consequences of that happening. Let's get something done before it is too late . . .

CHAPTER TEN

Players And Their Problems

A football manager must have a ruthless streak in his make-up if he is going to be a success. There has to be a time when, no matter what, the club must come first. If that means upsetting players or fans then so be it. You really have no choice in the matter.

When you look at the changes which have come in the game because of freedom of contract then it becomes even more apparent that you have to be able to act on possible transfers – either in or out – quickly and decisively. If someone becomes available then you go for him and sign him and if that means someone else has to drop out of the plans then that has to happen. You cannot allow your judgment as a manager to be affected by sentiment or by personal feelings. You can try to cushion any blows, try to soften them and try not to hurt anyone too much. But football is a game of change now more than it ever was before.

I doubt if any manager ever enjoys that part of the job which entails telling players they are no longer wanted. Or telling someone he has been left out of a Cup final team. Or being dropped from an important European match. But the job has to be done, at times. What you always hope is that while you are sitting in the office looking at the players' problems and trying to find the best way and the least hurtful way of telling someone they are dropped or transfer-listed or whatever, they are recognising your problems too.

Some of them do. Some of them don't. I always hope that a player understands the reasons for the decision I am making. I try to get my point of view over to them. It causes me a bit of worry but I can't allow it to worry me too much. My judgment is on the line – almost constantly on the line – and therefore tough decisions must be made.

You can't always be right – but what you have to do is to make the decisions for the right reasons. If they are obviously for the benefit of the team then no one can argue with you even if things might not work out.

There comes the time when some players have to move on. There is not a great deal you can do about that. Age or injury can affect careers. It happens everywhere, at any major club. While Graeme was still with the club we had to handle that type of situation when Terry Butcher left to go to Coventry. Now Terry had been a great servant to the club. Apart from that there was a strong sentimental tie with Terry, and with Chris Woods who left later, because they had been in at the start of all the major changes at Ibrox . . .

Terry was a proud player and he found it difficult to come to terms with things when Graeme dropped him from the first team. That was only natural. Knowing him over the years he spent at the club it was a reaction you had to expect. We felt that we had to make changes and Terry didn't see it our way – but we had to prevail. That was the only way the club could be run. I wish that one had happened under different circumstances because when Terry left he went under a bit of a cloud and that was not what anyone wanted. You are looking here at a player who had a pivotal role in re-shaping Rangers, a lad who captained us to that first so-important title win and a man whose name will go down as one of the finest captains Rangers have had. Now he comes back to the stadium and I think he realises, after his own stab at management, that often certain decisions have to be made which won't be popular with the players involved.

Players, after all, don't always see that their form has gone a bit. Or that, perhaps, their best days are behind them. Not many of them want to think that their career at the top is over. They don't want to accept that it's time for them to move, particularly if they are at a good club and have had a good relationship with the support at that club.

This is a problem we have at Rangers. No one wants to leave Ibrox because we have worked hard to create a good atmosphere here. I don't think you will ever find any player who will be able to complain about the way he has been treated at the club. The club policy in all the time I have been with Rangers is to look after the players, to treat them well and in that way you have a contented dressing-room, a happy work place and a group of players who all want to do their best for the club.

If you think that the particular mood you have worked hard to set up is being damaged or endangered in any way then you have to take quick action. I'm not suggesting that you can get a dressing-room where every one of a group of 20 boys likes each other. You'll never get that. But you have to have a general feeling of well-being in there. If the atmosphere is not right then you have to act. You cannot allow any problems which may manifest themselves off the field to ultimately cause problems on the field.

That's why I acted quickly over the Basile Boli affair when it had seemed initially that the player had criticised both myself and his fellow players in a French magazine interview.

The alleged remarks came after we had lost to AEK Athens in the preliminary round of the European Cup. The 'contents' of the article arrived in Scotland and there was an immediate storm. As I've said elsewhere in the book, anything concerning Rangers is always *big* news. This was no exception.

Basile was on the front pages and the back pages. He was suddenly the centre of attention and I ordered him back from France for an explanation. I was furious. When he arrived in the manager's office I told him that. I was ready to see him immediately. There was no way I wanted any kind of unrest or upset in the dressing-room. We had enough problems at that time with results. The last thing I needed was a row among the players – and it looked as if I was going to have that.

I was angry too at supposed suggestions that my own preparations had not been right for the game. It seemed a serious business. Until, that is, Basile began to offer his side of the story. None of the really bad remarks, he told me, had been in the article in France. He did not know where they had come from.

I told him to come back later that week with his lawyer to sort out the whole matter. He arrived, his lawyer with him, and with a translation of the now notorious article. When I read that I saw that Basile had been telling the truth. Some minor remarks he had made had been taken out of context. Others which had been used in Scotland were not in *France Football* at all.

It had been a storm in a teacup. But it showed the player the goldfish bowl existence we live at Ibrox. And it underlined to me once again the hype which abounds in football, both in Britain and in Europe. But, then, we have to live with it because it's that very hype which has pushed us on to centre stage in British football. And has boosted our reputation in Europe enough to sign players such as Basile Boli from Marseille and Brian Laudrup from Fiorentina. Both these players could have chosen other clubs ahead of us. Go back ten years in time, maybe even four or five years, and there is little doubt that they would have done. Basile had the chance to go to Paris St Germain or Spurs. Brian could have stayed in Italy or gone to two or three clubs in Spain or Germany.

It says a great deal for Rangers that we were able to attract them to Ibrox. When the Chairman and I sat down in the summer to look at the options we had we made a conscious decision to go for top foreign players, men with international reputations rather than local heroes if you like. It was an attempt to push the club onto another plateau. To give us that higher European profile that we want to have. Signing top names from Europe gives you added glamour and a great credibility. I think we started experiencing that when we brought in Mark Hateley from Monaco. Mark was one of the best signings made in the time Graeme and I were working together. Graeme had always wanted a powerful target man to lead the forward line. He had tried for Mark before and failed when he opted for Monaco as he left Milan. Then he was out injured for a lengthy spell but Graeme finally got his man in the summer of 1990 and Mark has repaid his one million pounds fee time and time again with the goals he has scored himself and those he has made for Coisty.

That same summer Graeme signed Oleg Kuznetsov and, again, that was a positive move in putting the club on the map. But that turned into a tragedy for the club. We had watched Oleg over a period of time and he had played against us for Dynamo Kiev in the European Cup. He was a quite exceptional player for that position because he had the touch and the passing skills and the vision of a midfield player. He was also the player who took all the free kicks for Kiev at a period when they were fielding just about the full Soviet Union international side. And then he collected that injury at Perth and he was never able to capture the same aggression or power that had always been a part of his game.

The club did everything possible for him. He was sent to the United States for the best medical care available for that type of injury. The particular operation he went through has become more commonplace in the game now but we were among the first clubs to have this done on players. Somehow or other, although the operations were successful, he could not regain the form which persuaded us to sign him. It was strange and it was tragic. We were bitterly disappointed from our own point of view but saddened for what had happened to Oleg. He just was not able to return to his previous high levels. The harder he tried to recapture that form the worse it all seemed to become for him. Eventually he moved to Israel but it was a loss to Rangers and to the Scottish game because Oleg Kuznetsov could have become a major personality in the Premier League.

Alexei Mikhailichenko, his fellow Ukrainian, made his own reputation in that Dynamo Kiev side and in the Soviet side which he skippered. He came to us from Sampdoria where he had had a spell in Italian football and he has as much ability as any player we have at Ibrox. The problem he has is that he has to go chasing the ball in Scottish football to get a touch and that isn't always the way he wanted to play. But in pure football terms when you look at his balance and his dribbling skills and his passing he is as good a player as you will see anywhere. But there is that little thing about him, that enigmatic bit, that you just never know when he is going to turn it on. Or just what he is going to do next. Yet he has scored some very important goals for us and he is, at times, a genius. OK, there are those fans who think that he is lazy but every player of his type can get landed with that tag. He just sees the game in a different way from how it is played in this country. There have been times when I have had to leave him out because I know I'm going to need a lad in the team who will work that little bit harder than Miko will. Yet he remains the type of player who can produce the unexpected, who will make that extra opening for you that no one else will, who will win you the game.

He is a personality player in a game which too often lacks personality. I find myself forgiving him a great deal when maybe he refuses to forage for the ball. Because there are other parts of the game he does brilliantly. He has his own pattern and style of play. You just have to accept that you are never going to change him. You can change clubs, change countries, but you are not going to change the way he thinks about the game and the way he wants to play it.

Again he helped to give us a better reputation internationally. Both he and Oleg told other players how big a club we were and how the players are treated and all of that helps when you are trying to go that little step further in becoming a European rather than just a Scottish club.

Andy Goram has been by far the best goalkeeper I have ever been involved with. He may just be the best goalkeeper I have ever seen. But that didn't stop us having our fall out at the end of last season.

Andy is a magnificent 'keeper. But when it comes to matters of fitness and discipline then that doesn't count for a lot. It's the same if I have to take action against a player who cost a signing-on fee or one who has cost a few million quid. They have to be treated the same. You don't let star players do things which other players are not allowed to do. Everyone is looked on in the same way.

So, when I felt that Andy's fitness levels had dropped I told him that he would be made available for transfer. I meant it, too. It was just that I thought he would not be as effective a goalkeeper while he was overweight. I knew that some of his training had been curtailed because of injuries and I knew the immense contribution he had made to the club but I had to take action and I did. And if necessary then I would have sold him . . .

But Andy took on board what I said to him at the end of the season. You can always speak to players and give them advice or give them a rollicking but you cannot always guarantee that they will listen to you. When they do and when they then take action to put things right it's a great feeling for any football club manager. That's how it happened with Andy. He came back for pre-season training more than a stone lighter than he had been. He worked very hard in the training we did at Ibrox and he continued that régime in il Ciocco. He played in the Ibrox tournament and looked as if he had never had any close season problems.

By the time we went to Athens I decided that he should come off the transfer list and fight for his place in goal. He could not have responded better than he did. Now he is back in our first team, back in the Scotland first team and playing as well as ever. Which is very well indeed!

It's always awkward for any manager to pick one or two players above all the others you have to deal with. But Andy, after an initial shaky spell, hit a superb seam of form. He found himself heavily criticised soon after joining Rangers from Hibs. It was hard for him to accept but, again, he had to learn just how much you are placed under the microscope at Rangers. When he picked up on that and settled in with the rest of the defence then he got to a level of performance which was unbelievable. For an 18-month spell I cannot recall a single error he made. You are looking at a goalkeeper here, someone whose slightest mistake is magnified. Yet I can't remember being able to blame Andy for one goal we lost in that spell. When he came for crosses he didn't miss a single one. They were either held or they were punched clear. His shot-stopping was uncanny and the way he stood up to players coming through on him in a one-on-one situation was better than any other 'keeper I have seen.

Then when the new pass-back rule came in and other 'keepers were being put under a lot of pressure, Andy handled that as if it had been the rule all along. In that time scale he proved himself a world-class goalkeeper. And it was nice to know that we had someone who was so professional and someone who surely ended all those English jeers and sneers about the goalkeeping standards in Scotland.

Later on, for me, it was a bonus when Andy got down to work again, got back to the fitness standards I demanded from him, and showed me that he wanted to stay at Ibrox. It's the kind of reaction you look for. And when it came I knew that we didn't have to worry about the goalkeeping position for a few years to come. Because, quite simply, we have the best there is. And he is staying . . .

Ian Durrant's injury was another major problem for all of us at Rangers. Even when he was a young boy he was producing the kind of football that set him apart from other players. I can remember Graeme saying to me that we would be lucky to hold on to him because Italian clubs would want to buy him in a few years' time. Then came the injury to Durranty up at Pittodrie and the operations and the convalescence and the months of special training as he tried to re-build his knee and regain his strength. This was a boy who had a talent few possessed. As far as I was concerned he was remarkably gifted, touched by greatness, and it was a tragedy that his career should have been interrupted so cruelly.

Ian Durrant had the greatest potential of any young player I have worked with. Now, often a talent which sparks, at times, when a player is young, dies away. Sometimes young lads don't realise their full potential. In Durranty's case he had reached football maturity while he was still a teenager. He had incredible vision even back then. And he was a lad who did everything instinctively. No one had to tell him what to do – he knew. He really did. This wasn't a cocky kid telling you he knew everything there was to know about the game – he had an instinctive understanding. His timing of runs into the box could not have been done any better by players of vast experience. And the number of times he found his way into the opposing box – for a midfield player it was phenomenal. Nor did he ever neglect his defensive duties. He would get up and down the field for you. It was a tragedy for the boy that he had to go through so much because given freedom from injury Ian Durrant would have been one of the football greats. I don't have the slightest doubt about that.

Of course, we have had so many outstanding players at the club over the eight-year spell. Richard Gough has shown tremendous qualities of leadership, taking over when Terry left. And there have been good solid professionals such as Nigel Spackman and Kevin Drinkell who might not have had long-term stays at Ibrox but who helped us win trophies while they were here.

Some of the more recent signings have not yet had time to settle in. Duncan Ferguson arrived for four million pounds and had to fight injury for most of his first season. Controversy has followed him and the fact that he was the most expensive signing in British football for some time didn't help him any. It brought him more attention than he needed . . . but now there are signs of the talent we all knew was there. I have no doubts at all that Duncan Ferguson will become a huge success with the club.

You have to remember that it was not the boy's fault that his value shot up to that massive amount of money. It was the going rate at that time. Leeds United had bid a couple of hundred thousand pounds less than we eventually paid. And we always knew that we would have to pay a premium on the player because his club, Dundee United, did not want to sell him to us as Premier League rivals. In the end we didn't pay all that much more than Leeds and we got the player we wanted.

Duncan was not bought to be pushed into the first team immediately. Our idea was always to allow him to get a taste of playing for Rangers, let him get a feel of the atmosphere at Ibrox and then use him sparingly to allow big Mark Hateley the occasional break from first team action. Things didn't quite happen that way – but that won't matter in the long run. Duncan is a tremendous investment for the club and he is Scottish, which is another bonus when you look at the European Union rules on foreign players.

It's a question, too, of investment in the future. If things work out for Duncan at Ibrox as I hope they do then Rangers will get ten or more years of football from the boy. And if we had delayed buying him then we could have missed out on what is a major Scottish-born talent. Also a few years down the road just what kind of money might you have to pay for a player with his attacking abilities? It was four million pounds just over a year ago. Chris Sutton went for a million more than that in the summer and so the transfer spiral continues upwards, ever upwards, and we have to be in there competing for the players we want.

You get back to criticism of buying players but I have made my justification for that policy in another chapter. And when you look around it's a policy which every big club has to adopt. Our aim by bringing in Brian and Basile is to show the bigger clubs in Europe that we were ready to invade their markets just as they are always prepared to do with us. Brian will be outstanding for us. His style of play, the way he dribbles with the ball, will appeal to Scottish fans. You don't have many out-and-out wingers now – even Brazil can't produce another Garrincha. But Brian is a player we will allow a lot of freedom and we expect him to attract a lot of people to the games we play. He is an entertainer.

Basile is another personality. He enjoyed a tremendous rapport with the French fans at his former club and I know that he would like to have the same relationship with the people at Ibrox. That could happen.

It is not easy for either player to just fit into our team or to become immediately accustomed to the pace of our game and the style of play in the Premier League. It's never been easy to adjust to all of that. And the demands on Rangers players are enormous. Players coming from England took time to get used to things. It's a more dramatic change for our two new lads. But when you buy experienced men with good pedigrees from Europe you know that, given time, it will all come out right.

The great thing for me is that the Chairman is always ready to back my judgment on those deals. We have a chat about what players might be out of contract, who would suit us and what they might cost and then we start talking to the players and clubs involved.

The Chairman is ambitious for the club. It's always said that he is not buying big name players just to win the Scottish championship. But we know at Ibrox that you have to win that to begin with – it's the passport into the big time. Basically, in the modern game, it's not managers who turn clubs into bigger clubs – Chairmen do that. You need the kind of driving force in the board room and we have it in David Murray.

He has never yet backed out of a deal. When we have needed players then he has found the money. He then deals with the major financial aspects of the transfer while I concentrate on making sure that the player is going to be happy with the club . . . Neither Laudrup nor Boli hesitated for very long – so we must be doing something right at Rangers!

These deals involving clubs from abroad are complex affairs and so, as I say, the Chairman looks after all of that. It isn't easy but he is there and he does it and I think it proves the value of having a man at the helm who owns the club. That's the way it has been in Italy for a long, long time and now we are having something the same in Britain. Jack Walker is at Blackburn and Alan Sugar at Spurs and we have David Murray and that trend will continue, I'm sure.

I don't think that Rangers would be sitting in the position they are in now without David Murray. He is a hands-on Chairman and with the money he has ploughed into the club that's only right. As long as David Murray remains as Chairman the club will continue to forge ahead. He won't stand still for a moment. We need another taste of European success on the pitch to go that next little stage . . .

One thing is certain: the dark days won't return to Ibrox. Whether I am still manager in a few years' time or not, the present policies will stay in place. Top players will be bought, the stadium will be constantly improved and the club will stay at the forefront of Scottish football. Too much work has been done to allow any of that to slip away.